WINE
TALK

A VINTAGE
COLLECTION OF
FACTS AND
LEGENDS FOR
WINE LOVERS

ANDREW JONES
The Flying Wine Man

PIATKUS

© 1996 Andrew Jones

First published in Great Britain by
Judy Piatkus (Publishers) Ltd
5 Windmill Street, London W1P 1HF

The moral right of the author has been asserted

A catalogue record for this book is
available from the British Library

Designed by Suzanne Perkins/Grafica
Illustrations by Rowan Barnes-Murphy

ISBN 0-7499-1697-4

Set in 11/14pt Frutiger Light by
Phoenix Photosetting, Lordswood, Chatham, Kent
Printed and bound in Great Britain by
Mackays of Chatham Plc, Lordswood, Chatham, Kent

Contents

Preface

I sincerely hope that reading this book will be as much fun as writing it. *Wine Talk* was never intended to turn anyone into a wine buff but rather to amuse, entertain and enlighten with facts, legends, anecdotes and stories from the world of wine which I have gathered in the course of two decades of travel and wine journalism.

Whilst I have made every effort to check, re-check and constantly update the information in the book, inevitably some of it may be superseded by the time it reaches the shelves. However be assured that the facts are true and correct to the best of my knowledge at the time of publication.

Andrew Jones

Curious Names

Bloody Good White and Bloody Good Red Easy drinking, everyday wines from the Bonny Doon winery in Santa Cruz, California, owned by the eccentric poet and winemaker Randall Grahm.

Brestnik A Bulgarian wine region that specialises in red wine from the grape varieties Merlot, Cabernet Sauvignon and the indigenous Mavrud.

Bulls Blood Two wines bear this name. The first, the Hungarian red Egri Bikavér, is the original source of the name, which dates back to 1552 when the Hungarian forces were besieged within the castle of Eger by the Turkish army of Ali Pasha. In a desperate last stand the local women served their men great draughts of Egri red wine to raise their spirits – then joined them to repel the Turkish onslaught. The Turks, being Muslims and abstainers, were mystified by the red wine on the beards of the Magyar force and are said to have believed rumours that their superhuman effort was possible only after they had drunk the warm blood of dead bulls.

The second wine is Torres Sangre de Toro from the Penedès region of Spain, and has obvious bullfighting connections.

A slight variation of the above is the Bulgarian red Bärenblut (Bears Blood) exported to Russia by the Svischtov winery. The producers realise that bears love anything sweet, so they add 10–15 grams of sugar per litre to suit the Russian palate.

Canary Not a yellow wine as wine quiz competitors have been known to suggest. Canary, sometimes called Canary Sack, was a fortified wine from the Canary Islands that was popular in Britain in the eighteenth and nineteenth centuries.

Château Boisson 'chateau drink'. A very small property in the Premières Côtes de Bordeaux that makes sweet white wine.

Château Carbonnieux This Grand Cru Classé from the Graves region is highly reputed for its fine white and red wines. It obtained its peculiar name when its proprietors, the Benedictine monks of Sainte-Croix Abbey, decided to sell their wines in the eastern Mediterranean and attracted some interest from a sultan in Constantinople. To get around the Muslim ban on the consumption of alcohol they identified the consignment as mineral water. As such it brought great praise from the sultan who is said to have remarked, 'How can these Christians drink wine when they have such delicious mineral water?'

Château Chasse-Spleen This Cru Exceptionnel from Moulis in the Bordeaux region has found many admirers for its fine red in recent years but its name defies translation. Even the great Bordeaux authority *Cocks et Feret* can only write, 'It matches perfectly with its name which means "chase-depression" and keeps its promise efficiently.' At best there is a suggestion that the vineyard is situated at a location where two soil formations meet causing a depression.

It is perhaps more amusing to learn that a director of this château was a Monsieur Merlot.

Château Guillotin A tiny property in the Puisseguin–Saint-Emilion appellation which proved rather unpopular in the latter part of the eighteenth century.

Domaine de la Caresse A small property in the Côtes de Castillon region of Bordeaux and a soft, gentle wine.

Dreikönigswein 'Three Kings' wine'. Before the 1971 German wine laws this term was used for an exceptionally late-picked wine, the grapes for which were left until 6 January, the Feast of the Three Kings. It did not guarantee sweetness levels.

Inferno A red wine pressed from Nebbiolo grapes in Valtellina, Italy.

Kanonkop This estate wine from Stellenbosch, South Africa bears a large gun on its label, commemorating a seventeenth-century cannon that was positioned on a nearby hillside and fired when ships entered Table Bay. Local farmers would set off with wagons laden with fresh produce to sell to the sailors or to exchange for other goods.

Landema Falls In March 1995 the Victoria Wine chain in Britain introduced a South African wine from the Coastal region. It could not be found in any wine book as it was a completely new blend with a carefully designed label. Its name, Landema Falls, referred to the large waterfall that was depicted on the label but whose existence was dubious. 'Landema' was simply an anagram of 'Mandela' – a clever marketing ploy.

Les Grenouilles 'The frogs'. A Grand Cru vineyard in Chablis of just under 10 hectares (25
acres). It is the happy home of noisy frogs.

Lollipop wine My name for a curious, Port-like,
fortified French wine called Maury from the
Pyrenées Orientales. It is aged out-of-doors in
large glass bottles, called *bons bons* whose necks

are covered in old tin cans to allow the wines to breathe but prevent insects entering. The leading producer is Mas Amiel.

Manicle A gripping wine that is an extremely rare blend of Chardonnay and Pinot Noir from the Bugey appellation in the Savoie region of France.

Moscato Curioso 'A light, tingling, frothing wine' made by Preston vineyards in the Dry Creek Valley of California's Sonoma region. Owner Lou Preston was determined to list an attractive Muscat wine. First he tried an Alsace-style dry Muscat but it failed to attract buyers. His second choice was not dissimilar to the popular fortified wine Muscat de Beaumes de Venise, but that too drew little response. The determined *vigneron* made one last attempt. This time he changed to an Asti style and commissioned artist Dian Zepeda to create a label that displayed 'the seductive quality of Muscat'. She supplied a curious cat design and the name Moscato Curioso. The result was an increasing stream of tourists and trade buyers demanding more and more. Subsequently, Lou can be seen most afternoons sitting in his rocking chair rubbing his paws and licking his whiskers.

Ottrott An Alsace village with a small number of vineyards and an identification problem.

Raimat Abadia A delicious Spanish red, a full-bodied blend of Tempranillo and Cabernet Sauvignon, that tells its own story through its name. At the top of its label is a small coat of arms showing a bunch of grapes, a hand and the date 1627. These were found on the keystone of a ruined castle on this Lerida estate when the Raventos family vineyard was being planted earlier this century. *Raim* is the Catalan word for 'grapes'. *Mat* means 'hand' and the symbols indicated that God would provide the gift of grapes but that it would take men to cultivate them. 'Abadia' refers to a small chapel that once belonged to the castle.

Refrigerator White and Refrigerator Red Basic Californian table-wine blends marketed in the 1980s by the now-liquidated Pat Paulsen Vineyards in Asti, Sonoma. Pat is the Hollywood comedian who achieved fame with the Smothers Brothers on United States national television. Some believe his personal style of humour was the root cause of many problems. The back label of Refrigerator White commented, 'Blessed with saucy impertinence, this wine's innate flushiness hints at a touch of benign resistance.'

Starboard Some might think Andrew Quady's Californian alternative to Port carries wine's silliest name but it is his tongue-in-cheek protest against the international regulations that forbid him to use the word 'Port'. Guests are always encouraged to pass the Starboard two to the right and one to the left.

Twin Peaks This Bulgarian red wine has no connection with the popular television series but is a direct translation of *Dve Mogli*, 'two hills', the name of a village in the Rousse region of northeast Bulgaria where this most attractive, oak-aged Cabernet Sauvignon is produced.

Vigne de L'Enfant Jesus This must be the most privileged name of all. It is a single-estate red Burgundy in the Beaune-Grèves appellation belonging to Bouchard Père et Fils. Its origin is believed to lie with some Carmelite sisters in Beaune and the label displays a processional figure of the infant Christ.

Colourful Characters

Angas, George Fife Almost certainly one of the few total abstainers whose name is displayed on a successful wine label – Angas Brut Australian sparking wine, whose rosé has a large following. Born in Newcastle-on-Tyne in 1789, Angas was a director of the South Australia Company, which was responsible for the initial land distribution in the colony. He was a prominent Baptist, a director of the Sunday School Union and a keen advocate of temperance. His memory is honoured in the naming of the town of Angaston in the Barossa Valley and its largest winery, Yalumba, understandably chose his name for their bubbly.

Babich, Josip (Joe) Dalmatian-born founder of the celebrated New Zealand winery. In 1914 he opened the only gum-field winery ever known. (A gum-field can be likened to a coal-field. Gum trees shed their gum which then hardens as a resin in the soil. Years later this resin may be dug out of the gum-field and used for varnishes, lacquers and linoleum.) It was at Kaikino and also had the most northerly vineyard ever recorded on New Zealand soil. Babich was prosecuted for selling too little wine to a Maori – the law required a minimum volume of 2 gallons (9 litres) – but secured the services of H.H. Ostler, a future judge of the Supreme Court, and was cleared. In 1919 he founded the Babich winery in the Henderson Valley near Auckland.

Bernard de Got In 1300, as Archbishop of Bordeaux, Bernard de Got built the first ever wine château in a vineyard that his brother had donated to the Church. It was in the Graves region where the land was covered in small gravel. This property was later named Château Pape-Clément after Bernard was elected Pope Clement V in 1305.

In 1309, during the 'Babylonian Exile', he took up residence in Avignon and whilst there went in search of a site for a summer palace. Instead he chose land covered in pebbles, for a second and new (neuf) wine chateau. He died just five years later and it was another 30 years before the project, which became known as Chateauneuf-du-Pape, was completed.

Bernhardt, Sarah The nineteenth-century actress shocked Parisian society in the Naughty Nineties when she was photographed naked in a bath of Perrier-Jouët Champagne.

Bohemund II, archbishop and elector of Trier This much-loved fourteenth-century prelate was apparently lying on his deathbed in Landshut Castle with no hope of recovery when a gift of wine from Bernkastel, said to have medicinal properties, arrived. It was given to the failing archbishop who fell into a deep sleep and woke the next morning restored to good health. Such was the acclaim for this miraculous cure that the vineyard was named the Bernkasteler Doktor and to this day its wine is generally considered to be one of the finest sweet whites made. Ironically, only red wine was produced there in the fourteenth century.

Brown, George Massiot In 1928 this Scottish poster artist, reputedly inspired by the character of Zorro played by Douglas Fairbanks Senior in *The Gaucho*, sketched a shadowy silhouette which was sold to the house of Sandeman for 50 guineas. Named 'The Don', it became the most widely recognised wine logo in the world.

Charlemagne The outstanding white Burgundy appellation of Corton-Charlemagne is named after this eighth-century emperor. Legend relates that he was responsible for the introduction of Chardonnay vines into Corton.

For many years, it is said, he owned red wine vineyards in the region but as he grew older his beard turned white and his wife began to complain about the droplets that clung to it. So he instructed that new white vines should be planted and soon his wife's chiding was a thing of the past.

Clarence, Duke of History relates that when the Duke of Clarence was sentenced to death in 1477 he was allowed to select the method of his execution. His choice was to be drowned in a butt of Malmsey wine.

Clicquot, Nicole Barbe Better known as la Veuve, or the widow, Clicquot. At the age of 28 she inherited a small but growing Champagne house in Reims when her husband died prematurely in 1806. It later adopted her name. She is credited with the invention of the *remuage*, or riddling process, after an incident when she ordered her cellar carpenter to chisel a series of holes in her best dining-room table. This eventually led to the *pupitre* system whereby Champagne bottles, angled at 45 degrees, are inserted in hinged wooden boards. Over a six-to-eight-week period the bottles are turned and inverted causing the sediment to slide down the neck and into the crown cork. The necks of the bottles are then frozen and the ice pellet containing the sediment is removed.

Champagne Veuve Clicquot non-vintage remains one of the finest amongst the Grande Marque houses.

Dom Pierre Pérignon The cellar master of the abbey of Hautvillers from 1668 to 1715. Clearly Dom Pérignon did not invent Champagne, as has been suggested by some, but he was a major influence in the early years of the wine's development. His use of strengthened London bottles and Portuguese corks substantially reduced losses through breakage and oxidation. Within the Champagne region he was probably most widely recognised for his development of blending and his knowledge of viticulture. He is remembered by the prestige label of Champagne Moët et Chandon: Dom Pérignon.

Duffour-Dubergier, Sadi Few people will know his name but many will know his work. Mayor of Bordeaux and president of its Chamber of Commerce, Duffour-Dubergier became the chairman of the 1855 committee that officially classified the Grand Cru Classé wines of Bordeaux. Although it is occasionally argued that the list should be re-assessed, it is remarkable how accurate a guide the classification continues to be.

Evans, Len Veteran, Welsh-born Australian wine expert and entrepreneur, widely acknowledged as an outstanding taster and wine writer – accolades that are quite an achievement for a man whose initial career was as a golf professional.

Forrester, Baron James Dynamic and inspirational leader of the Port trade who met a mysterious death in 1861 at the age of 51. He was the first to prepare navigational charts for the dangerous Douro river which flows through Spain and Portugal, but nevertheless drowned in it when his *barco rabelo* capsized following a generous lunch hosted by the equally colourful Doña Antonia Ferreira. Rumours persist that he was dragged to the bottom by large boots and a money-belt full of gold. Recent evidence indicates that his body may have been found by Romanies working on the construction of a railway line, who took the gold and buried the baron, mafia-style, in the base of a new bridge at Pinhao.

Frescobaldi, Berto In 1310 he was appointed crown counsellor to Edward II of England. In their capacity as bankers the florentine family lent Edward I and Edward II a total of £150,000 to fight the Scottish wars against William Wallace (Braveheart) and Robert the Bruce. They were also official Inspectors and Receivers of Taxes for England.

Among other benefits this gave the Marchesi

de Frescobaldi the opportunity to start shipping their wines to England where the charming Chianti Rufina Riserva from their 1000-year-old Castello di Nipozzano remains a firm favourite.

Gramp, Johann A devout but illiterate Lutheran who emigrated from Bavaria to South Australia in 1837 when just 17 years old. Ten years later he travelled to the Barossa Valley to join a Lutheran settlement called Bethany. Apparently inspired by the ripeness of the few rows of vines they had planted for sacramental purposes, Johann obtained a land grant alongside a tiny stream called Jacob's Creek. There, in 1847, he planted 4 acres (1.6 hectares) of vines and built a small winery that still survives and of course founded a name that has since become known around the globe.

Guestier, Daniel The founder of the Bordeaux negociant, Barton et Guestier. Guestier con-structed a special armed *balahow* (a large sailing ship, see 'Winespeak' **Grand Nancy**) in order to penetrate the British naval blockade of France and supply wine to boost the morale of George Washington's army during the War of American Independence. Subsequently B&G wines are widely found in the United States but only occa-sionally seen in Britain.

Heggie, Colin 'Oscar' A robust Australian horse-man after whom the popular Heggie's Vineyard is named. Before settling on the land which today bears his name, he led a semi-nomadic existence taking files of chained prisoners from Darwin to Adelaide for sentencing. On one occasion he was so convinced of the innocence of a small group that he set them free and, after a discreet lapse in time, reported that they had escaped. The sketch on the Eden Valley winery's label depicts him on one of his nightly visits to the Valley Hotel in Angaston, where he would ride into the bar and drink his beer while mounted, depending on his horse to take him home.

Johnson, Dr Samuel The eminent man of letters who was also a gourmand. According to James Boswell, his biographer, he often enjoyed two bottles of Port with his meal. Although this was a generous allowance, the bottles were pint measures and Port in the eighteenth century was not fortified. On some occasions, however, Dr Johnson was known to add sugar and brandy to make his own fortified version.

Klaebisch, Otto Known as the 'Champagne Führer' from 1940 to 1944, he was responsible for the movement of every single bottle of the wine during the German occupation of the Champagne region. He had close connections with the von or de Mumm family who seized back the famous Mumm Champagne house in 1940, having been dispossessed of it following the Treaty of Versailles in 1919. Both Klaebisch and the von Mumms left hastily in 1944 as the Allies approached. After the war Otto worked as the manager of Matheus Muller Sekt owned by Godefroy de Mumm; its wines were a sad disappointment compared with his wartime tipple.

Lindeman, Dr Henry John Australian wine pioneer born in Surrey, England, who as a student-surgeon at St Bartholomew's Hospital, London, was a contemporary of Christopher Penfold. Both men emigrated, quite independently, to Australia where they settled 600 miles (965 kilometres) apart. Here they established themselves as general practitioners and prescribed wine – which they provided from their own vineyards – for its medicinal benefits. Dr Lindeman planted his first vines at Cawarra in the Hunter Valley in 1843. (See also **Penfold, Dr Christopher Rawson**.)

Marqués de Monistrol Nineteenth-century Catalan aristocrat and sparkling wine pioneer who restored the eighth-century monastic vineyards of San Sadurni d'Anoia. He concluded that his full name of Don José Maria Escriva de Romani Y Dusay, Marqués de Monistrol Y de Aguillar was a trifle long for his labels so abbreviated his title to Marqués de Monistrol.

Mau, Yvon Nonagenarian Bordeaux merchant whose silhouette on a penny-farthing is on his company's back labels. It recalls the time when he developed a substantial business in the region by cycling from vineyard to vineyard and from customer to customer, a mode of transport which, along with wine, has apparently lengthened his life span.

Mirassou, Pierre Californian wine pioneer and founder, in 1854, of America's oldest continuously operated winery: Mirassou Vineyards. He is best remembered for saving the precious French noble vine cuttings that he was shipping to San José. Having rounded Cape Horn, their survival was put at risk by water rationing. Mirassou purchased the ship's entire stock of potatoes, slit each one and placed a vine cutting in it. This procedure was also used to good effect by immigrants to the southern hemisphere.

Munson, Thomas Volnay Oklahoma-born horti-culturist who, in 1876, commenced vineyard trials at Denison, Texas, which eventually helped to defeat the phylloxera that was wiping out the vines of France. He was the first to graft French cuttings successfully on to resistant American rootstock and worked with the French govern-ment who in 1888 honoured him with the title Chevalier du Mérite Agricole.

Murphy, Paddy Irish horse dealer and founder, in 1730, of what later became known as the house of Domecq which is now absorbed into the giant Allied-Domecq group. He was one of several Irish livestock traders who were attracted to Andalucia in the eighteenth century. His succes-sors sold the Sherry business to the Basque-born Pedro Domecq two generations after Murphy had established it.

Nelson, Admiral Horatio Owner of a vineyard in Marsala, Sicily, a reward from Ferdinand IV and Queen Carolina of the Two Sicilies for protecting their country against the Napoleonic forces. The shrewd admiral persuaded George III that the British navy should be supplied with 500 pipes of the fortified wine annually, the equivalent of 282,000 bottles. Ironically, Marsala was used for the victory toast at the battle of Trafalgar as Nelson lay breathing his last.

Pasteur, Louis The celebrated nineteenth-century Arbois chemist who developed pasteurisation through experiments that involved various local wines. He identified oxidation and explained its destructive process. Pasteurisation is still used for many inexpensive wines sold in bottles that are not sealed with corks. Pasteur also isolated the micro-organisms in yeast that cause fermentation.

Penfold, Dr Christopher Rawson A general practitioner born in Sussex, England, who settled at Magill, nowadays a suburb of Adelaide, South Australia, in 1844. There he built the historic Grange Cottage, which has recently been restored, and prescribed wine from the adjoining vineyard for his ailing patients. Penfolds Grange is widely considered to be the finest red wine in the southern hemisphere. (See also **Lindeman, Dr Henry John**.)

Riddoch, John Scots-born Australian politician and benefactor who, when he retired in 1891, founded the Coonawarra Fruit Colony, a land project in which he guaranteed to purchase all the grapes grown. Acting on the advice of a humble gardener called William Wilson, a fellow Scot, Riddoch selected a long strip of *terra rossa* soil that lay on top of limestone. Riddoch died in

1901 but had the pleasure of seeing the first great vintage. Sadly, his family did not share his enthusiasm and after his death the project was allowed to crumble. Only one man, Bill Redman, persisted, and for half a century he alone produced reds there. Two wines, Redman and Rouge Homme are named after him. Today the judgement of Riddoch and Redman is recognised in what many consider Australia's finest red wine region.

Robertson, John 'Poor Man' An extremely wealthy Coonawarra sheep farmer after whom the excellent Robertson's Well Cabernet Sauvignon is named. In the 1840s he sunk one of the first deep wells in the area, breaking through the limestone layer beneath the *terra rossa* soil, the two most significant geological factors that influence the prime vineyards in the region. His nickname arose because he never owned fewer than 60,000 sheep.

Schubert, Max The late, head winemaker for Penfold's who, during the 1950s, fought against his own directors to develop Grange Hermitage, acknowledged by many as a truly outstanding red wine and by some as the finest in the Southern hemisphere. Quite clearly he showed the rest of the wine world that Australia could make a truly great, long-lasting wine and left a legacy that both old colleagues and former competitors respect.

Spitting Bill The nickname wine experts have given to a leading Chablis producer who is capable of showering them from a distance of 2 metres (6½ feet). He remains anonymous in order not to detract from the merit of his superb wines.

Tchelistcheff, André Russian-born, French-trained winemaker who was a major influence on the development of Cabernet Sauvignon in the Napa Valley in California. Born in the heyday of imperialist Russia, he studied agronomy at the Pasteur Institute in Paris before gaining winemaking experience in Burgundy. In France he met Georges de Latour who was responsible for persuading him to go to the Napa Valley to make great red wine. This he did from 1936 to 1973 at Beaulieu Vineyard, where he established Georges de Latour Private Reserve as the first great Californian red. Interviewed at 90 years of age, when he was re-commissioned as a consultant by Beaulieu Vineyard, he said, 'There is never a status quo with wine and that is what I have always believed.' He died in 1994 and remains a great influence on wine professionals who knew him.

Tio Pepe Uncle Joe, or Tio Pepe in Spanish, was a real figure, whose love for, and care of, his frail, sickly nephew resulted in his name being recorded for posterity on this most popular of Fino Sherries. When the father of the infant Manuel Gonzales Angel died early in the nineteenth century and left his widow with seven children to raise, Uncle Joe became guardian of Manuel, who was not expected to survive. He took the boy into his home in Seville and raised him as his own. He was rewarded by the sight of his nephew gradually gaining strength. Years later, when the prosperous Manuel set up a small

Sherry house, he named his uncle's favourite blend of crisp dry Fino Sherry after him.

van Riebeeck, Jan See 'Firsts'

Vatchkov, Marko In 1909 this village school-teacher persuaded seven friends to join him in the first-ever Bulgarian wine co-operative, Gamza at Suhindol. They pooled their resources and funded a one-year study programme for Marko in Bordeaux, where he visited many French co-operatives and took careful notes of their designs and methods.

On his return to Suhindol membership of the co-operative increased to 50 and a winery, mod-elled on those Marko had seen in south-west France, was erected. Today his statue overlooks a beautiful garden set amidst what later became one of the first private-enterprise wineries in the country. His inspiration led the way for many of Bulgaria's remarkable red-wine bargains.

Watson, Jimmy The most prestigious Australian wine trophy, given annually for the best one-year-old red at the Melbourne Wine Show. It is named after the late restaurateur and expert who did much to encourage competition among winemak-ers. Only one producer, Wolf Blass, has ever won the award three years running.

Notable Wine Publicity

the Mercier barrel Eugène Mercier occurs twice in this section because of his talent and showmanship. His greatest feat was to exhibit a 20 ton Champagne barrel at the 1889 Paris Centennial, held to celebrate the 100th anniversary of the French Revolution. Champagne Mercier stole the show from its many rivals with what appeared to be a carefully prepared stunt, but one that nevertheless quickly ran into trouble. For 20 years Eugène planned the construction of a gargantuan wine cask with a capacity of 200,000 bottles, said to have been made from '250 one-hundred-year-old oak trees'. Unfortunately, he had overlooked transport arrangements and when the time came for the barrel to make the eight-day journey from Épernay to Paris problems arose.

The cask, mounted on a wooden chassis with four enormous wheels, was drawn by a team of 24 oxen and yet just a few miles from the Mercier cellars 18 horses had to be added to haul it up a hill. The next incident occurred when the road between several small houses was too narrow for it to pass. Eugène Mercier simply bought the properties offering sufficiently generous terms to gain immediate vacant possession, and demolished them.

Eventually the cask neared the gates of Paris but there was insufficient space for it to pass beneath them. An emergency request to remove the gates was made to the Minister of War and finally – and with considerable triumph – the Mercier Champagne barrel arrived at the exhibition amidst a most welcome glare of publicity. The exercise had been expensive but the sales of Mercier reached fizzy new heights and all proved worthwhile.

the Mercier balloon Encouraged by the results of his 1889 promotion, Eugène Mercier decided to seek further, but less expensive publicity, in Paris the following year.

He hired a hot-air balloon with a pilot, secured it against railings in the Champs de Mars and invited passers-by to climb aboard and enjoy free Champagne. For several days the exercise proceeded smoothly until a sudden squall arose and the balloon tore free of its moorings and hurtled over the rooftops of Paris. Nine astonished passengers, a waiter and the pilot hung on for dear life. The balloon rushed onwards in an easterly direction and soon passed over the Champagne region; it was steadily gaining altitude and its occupants feared the worst. Sixteen hours later it landed remarkably intact in a forest in Alsace, then under German annexation. The police arrived and Champagne Mercier was threatened with prosecution for illegal immigration. It soon became apparent that the case could not be proven and only a minor charge was brought: Mercier was fined 20 crowns for failing to declare six untouched bottles of Champagne found on the balloon which the travel-sick passengers had rejected.

The publicity produced headlines around the world and Eugène Mercier stated that it was the cheapest publicity the house had ever achieved,

costing 'less than a centime a line'. He did not repeat the exercise.

the Codorníu procession In 1872 Codorníu produced the first Spanish sparkling wine by what was then called the Champagne-method. Several years later, in 1885, the Codorníu chairman, Manuel Raventos, decided to introduce it to the

Barcelona market. He was anxious that the new style should receive the maximum publicity. Codorníu already enjoyed substantial trade in parts of Catalonia where its wines were delivered door-to-door by horse-drawn wagons. So it simply took advantage of this method of delivery.

At that time the main business centre of Barcelona was a maze of ancient, long, narrow streets which created such transport problems that only one-way traffic was permitted. One day, just before the morning rush hour, several dozen newly decorated Codorníu carts began deliberately travelling against the traffic flow and immediately created chaos, bringing everything to a standstill.

The company was heavily fined but was happy to settle its dues, for nobody could possibly have missed the stunt and newspapers carried the Codorníu name in banner headlines. It was never admitted, but rumour suggested, that matters were eased by the generous distribution of free samples of what was called 'the first Spanish Champagne'.

G. H. Mumm's Cordon Rouge When it was announced that the first American Centennial Exhibition would be held in Philadelphia in 1876 many major Champagne houses were keen to be present, as the American market had considerable potential. The problem for Champagne exhibitors was how to attract attention ahead of their competitors.

Mumm's representative in Paris, an agent called Welby Jourdan, discussed the matter with his father whose immediate advice was to decorate Mumm bottles with the cordon rouge, the red ribbon of France's highest honour: the Légion d'Honneur. Jourdan, a most energetic promoter, sent for some red silk ribbon the next day, cut it and tied it to a bottle of Mumm Champagne and recommended the idea to his directors. His suggestion was gratefully accepted and resulted in notable success for Mumm in the United States. Eventually sales grew to such a degree that wrapping the bottles by hand became impractical and a label with a printed ribbon was designed.

Théophile Roederer's Cristal bottle In 1864 two brothers, Gustave and Léon Bousigues, hatched a conspiracy with a humble character from Alsace called Théophile Roederer. Their intention was to use his name to start a Champagne house that would woo trade away from the long-established house of Louis Roederer. They began by launching their first bottles simply labelled Champagne Roederer, in Reims. This threw the market into confusion and the brothers were immediately hauled before the courts who decreed that their labels must display the name Théophile in front of Roederer, along with a foundation date of 1864.

This soon put paid to the brothers' schemes in northern France so they headed for imperialist Russia, Louis Roederer's most important market. There, generous quantities of heavily sweetened Champagne were drunk in the court of Alexander II but nobody seemed able to monopolise the Tsar's official order. French law was void on Russian soil and so it was possible for the

Bousigues once again to use labels that read
Champagne Roederer.

When the brothers heard that Alexander was
interested in finding an exclusive *cuvée* – blend of
Champagne – they put into effect their most
enterprising ploy yet. Apparently the Tsar had
complained that when a napkin covered most of
the bottle it was impossible for his courtiers to
distinguish between one label and another. Once
they had obtained a reasonable volume of business from the court, Léon and Gustave returned
to Reims and made discreet enquiries about bottle
production. They sought a unique example that
would be immediately recognisable and eventually
found a glassworks in Flanders that agreed to
make a few hand-crafted, clear white crystal bottles. They showed these to their most important
customer, who was so delighted that Théophile
Roederer Cristal became his exclusive Champagne
and received widespread exposure.

For nearly 30 years the impostor house blos-
somed and profited from trade across Eastern
Europe and Asia. The Cristal bottle became a
talking-point and the Champagne was the most
prestigious in Russia, the biggest export market

that the wine has ever known. But uncharted problems arose in the 1890s and by 1896 trade had declined seriously. The company was placed in liquidation and sold to a Monsieur Aubert. Eventually, in 1904, after many attempts, Léon Olry-Roederer, the head of the injured Champagne Louis Roederer, acquired the Théophile Roederer company and assumed the rights for Cristal. A little later the labels were reprinted: the name Louis replaced Théophile while Roederer remained intact.

Théophile Roederer Cristal was so heavily sweetened that nobody could have known whether the Champagne was of the finest quality or of the humblest standard – which many suspect it was. Today, however, Louis Roederer Cristal has a justifiably fine reputation.

Mayor of Asti (Sonoma, California) In 1986 when Clint Eastwood was elected mayor of Carmel-by-the-Sea amidst much hullabaloo, wine producer and former Hollywood comedian Pat Paulsen seized the opportunity for a copy-cat spoof event that he hoped would attract nationwide attention to his winery.

A photograph of Pat holding a pitchfork 'American Gothic-style in front of Asti City Hall' was circulated to the press and a July inauguration was planned, to which scores of mayors and dignitaries from neighbouring towns were invited, along with a jazz band and a Ronald Reagan impersonator. Television teams and floods of journalists arrived and the story was seen, read and heard across North America, but all to little avail. Pat Paulsen Vineyards failed, leaving some people wondering whether the best publicity in the world is any use if the wine is produced by a comedian.

Extremes

most northerly The Neuenahr Kirchtürmchen in the Ahr region of Germany is at approximately 51°N. Surprisingly, this region is best known for its red wines.

nearest to the Equator The Guder Winery is situated 1,000 kilometres (625 miles) north of the Equator, east of Addis Ababa in Ethiopia at 9°N 39°E. Its results are not said to be exciting. Another near Equatorial example is the Tacama Vineyard near Ica, Peru at 14°S 75°W. It is 1760 kilometres (1100 miles) south of the Equator. Vines were first planted in Peru by the Spanish missionary Francesco de Carabantes in 1566. East of the Atlantic, a notable example must be the vineyard of the attractive Indian sparkling wine Omar Khayyám at 19.07°N 74°E at Narayangon in the Pune district of Maharashtra. It is situated at an altitude of about 760 metres (2500 feet) in the Sahyadri mountains near Bombay approximately 2010 kilometres (1250 miles) north of the Equator.

most southerly The Black Ridge winery at Alexandra in the Central Otago region on the South Island of New Zealand is situated just below latitude 45°.

highest altitude vineyard (for commercial production) La Florida Estate of the Arnaldo Etchart company near Cafayate in the Salta province of north-west Argentina is at 1695 metres (5560 feet). It comprises 303 hectares (750 acres) and specialises with white Torrontés grapes. It also has Chardonnay, Malbec, Merlot and Cabernet Sauvignon. Its annual rainfall of about 150–200 millimetres (6–8 inches) is often provided by just a couple of storms. Etchart Cafayate Torrontés 1993 was named White Wine of the Year 1994 at the International Wine Challenge in London, to the surprise of many experts who did not even know the grape variety.

highest altitude winery (for non-commercial production) The Australian winery Taltarni is involved in a joint venture with the government of the Himalayan kingdom of Bhutan. Two small vineyards have been planted near Paro and Thimpu at approximately 2200 metres (7200 feet) and the first production is expected in 1998. However, the wine will be used chiefly for state occasions and will not be available to the general public.

smallest French Appellation Château-Grillet in the northern Rhône valley consists of just 2.3 hectares (5½ acres) and has an average annual production of around 12,000 bottles. Its fine dry white wine is at its best when drunk at around 18–24 months.

smallest French Appellation production This is the fortified wine Rasteau Rancio, from the village of Rasteau in the southern Rhône valley. It is made solely by the tiny family house of Emile Bressy who sometimes make only one *barrique* (225 litres/49½ gallons) a year. The wine is aged in oak for a minimum of seven years.

largest vineyard ownership In 1978 the respected Californian wine journalist Robert Lawrence Balzar recorded that Almadén Vineyards in California owned '15,000 acres (6070 hectares) in four counties' and possessed '35,000 oak barrels'. The figure has subsequently been reduced.

largest English vineyard Denbies Vineyard at Woking in Surrey. Owned by Adrian White, it has 107.2 hectares (265 acres) under vines.

largest pressing (crush) operation In the 1994 vintage the Glen Ellen winery based in Sonoma, California, operated 27 separate pressing sites throughout the state. Altogether it handled 87,867 tons of noble grape varieties. Over 12 million bottles of Chardonnay and 12 million bottles of White Zinfandel were produced. Glen Ellen is the biggest-selling Chardonnay in the world.

the largest automatic *remuage* (riddling) operation The mammoth Seaview sparkling wine cellar in Victoria, Australia is home to an awesome display of computer-controlled, bottle-turning power. Known as 'BAS' or the 'Big Aussie Shakers' there are 42 giant giro-pallets, each of which contains eight crates holding 504 bottles each. 'BAS' takes just three days to shake the sediment into the necks of the 169,344 bottles prior to its removal, compared with six to eight weeks if manipulated by hand.

fastest planted vineyard Claimed by the Richmond Grove Cowra Vineyard. In just under 12 months in 1989, a total of 242 hectares (605 acres) was planted in 56 separate blocks using laser technology.

greatest number of family members involved In 1993 Don McWilliam, head of the Australian winemaking dynasty of that name, claimed that his company was able to field a 13-man rugby team limited to members of the family who bore the McWilliam name and who worked full-time within the organisation. On closer examination the figures were confirmed, but several 'players' were considered to be of an age where

34

they should be restricted to running the line or cleaning the boots.

the only teetotal winemaker in the world(?) Bill Calabaria of West End Wines at Griffith in New South Wales, Australia, is apparently allergic to wine and so looks, noses, swirls and spits but never swallows!

highest price paid for a bottle of wine in auction at Christie's, New York A record US $112,500 was paid for a case of Chateau Mouton-Rothschild 1945 at the Zachys-Christie's sale of 13 April 1996 in New York. This was the equivalent of $1,562.50 a glass.

highest price paid for a case of wine in auction at Christie's, London One dozen Romanée-Conti 1978 brought £46,400 on 8 August 1995.

record value for any individual wine auction at Christie's, London On 16 June 1994 the contents of an anonymously owned 'magnificent private cellar' were sold for £1,564,200.

Firsts

first vineyard Claims for Erivan, Armenia, near the base of Mount Ararat are not indepentently proven although Genesis 9, 20 records that 'Noah began the planting of vineyards'. The late Dr Konstantin Frank, a Ukranian-born viticultural authority, believed that the white Rkatsiteli grape variety originated there. However, biblical scholars can only speculate a flood date of 5000–4000 BC while 7000–5000 BC is the earliest carbon dating of cultivated grape pips from the Republic of Georgia. It is assumed these came from wine production.

first recorded vineyard in Europe It is impossible to establish this with any certainty but in about 1000 BC Homer recommended the wines of Thrace (modern southern Bulgaria) as a prolific source of attractive, good value reds – a situation that continues to this day.

Recent rumours from Moldova of 6000-year-old vineyards are as yet unproven.

first vineyard in England It is generally believed that the Romans first planted vines in England but no specific evidence has survived. The Venerable Bede wrote in AD 731 that 'vines are cultivated in various localities' which suggests that viticulture was a long-standing tradition. *Domesday Book*, in its survey of England between 1080 and 1086, recorded 46 vineyards at sites including Kensington, Westminster and Holborn. Ely in today's Cambridgeshire was the most northerly.

first vineyard in Wales The twelfth-century
monk Geraldis Cambrensis wrote that his father, a
Norman baron, had a vineyard at his castle at
Manorbier, Pembrokeshire.

first vineyard in Scotland The Scottish climate
has not yet proved to be sufficiently hospitable
for the consistent cultivation of vines, but in the
early 1920s a bizarre attempt was made near
Galashiels with a 1.6 hectare (4 acre) vineyard
entirely under glass.

first vineyard in Ireland Again we depend on
the Venerable Bede, who wrote 'there is no lack
of vines'.

first attempt to plant vines in the New World Christopher Columbus made an unsuccessful planting in the Lesser Antilles during his second voyage in 1493.

first wine shipped to the New World On that same voyage, to Puerto Rico, in 1493 Columbus carried butts of Sherry as ballast. It is inconceivable that the contents were not tasted on arrival.

first vineyard in the New World In 1519 the Spanish conquistador Hernando Cortés recorded the planting of the first vineyard across the oceans at Parras in Mexico by Captain Francisco de Urdinola. In 1524 Cortés instructed all *los encomenderos* (landowners) to plant ten vines for every dead Indian!

first vineyard within today's United States The Franciscan fathers Garcia Zuniga and Juan de Salazar planted Spanish Mission vines at the Señora del Guadalupe Mission at El Paso, Texas, in 1659. Earlier attempts had been made in Virginia but failed.

first wine made in North America Jean Ribault, a French sea captain, and some 50 of his men, were not impressed with the results they achieved when they crushed the grapes of indigenous wild vines near St Augustine, Florida, in 1562.

first recorded planting of noble varieties in California The aptly named Jean-Louis Vignes from Cadillac in the Bordeaux region planted noble varieties at El Aliso Ranch, near the site of the modern Union Station in Los Angeles, in 1833.

first vineyard in the southern hemisphere Roman Catholic missionaries and other pioneer settlers in South America often planted vines for sacramental wine. The first recorded cultivation was in 1548 at Copiapo, Chile, by the Spanish conquistador Francisco de Aguirre. In the Argentine the Jesuit father Cedron planted a vineyard at Cuyo in 1556. Some writers suggest earlier cultivation in Peru but the first recorded date is 1566 for a vineyard established at Ica by the Spanish missionary Francesco de Carabantes.

first vineyard in South Africa This was planted in 1652 by Jan van Riebeeck, the founder of the first Dutch colony in what is now Cape Town. Three years later he uttered words that have become part of South African history: 'Today, praise be to God, wine was pressed for the very first time'. Van Riebeeck used wine both in Holy Communion and to protect sailors against scurvy.

first vineyard in Australia The eminent Australian wine historian, Dr Philip Norrie, has established that this was planted in Sydney Cove in 1788 by Governor Philip.

first vineyard in New Zealand An experimental vineyard with many different grape varieties was planted at Kerikeri in 1819 by Samuel Marsden, an Anglican missionary.

first sparkling wine in the world The first recorded bottle-fermented wine was made at the Benedictine monastery of Saint-Hilaire at Limoux in the Aude region of France. It is dated at 1531, some 137 years before Dom Pérignon commenced his activities at Hautvillers in the Champagne region, and was a forerunner of Blanquette de Limoux.

first Champagne In London sparkling 'Champaign' was produced as early as 1630. Molasses was poured into barrels of still white wine from the Marne region causing a secondary fermentation.

first Brut Champagne in the world This was shipped to England by Perrier-Jouët in 1864.

first late-picked sweet wine Such wines may have been produced for centuries before records were kept. The earliest date so far proven is 1526 in Neusiedlersee, Austria, when it was part of Hungary. However, the production of sweet wines might have been a regular practice in the Tokay region of Hungary even earlier; in 1939 it was reported that Fukier, a wine merchant in Warsaw, Poland, possessed 328 bottles of 1606 Tokay Aszú. The oldest Tokay vintage known to have survived is a 1670 bottle in Tolcsva Museum. Late picking was not recorded in Germany until 1775, at Schloss Johannisberg.

first Port house The tradition of wine-making is centuries old in the Port wine region but the great tradition of Port houses began in 1670 when Warre & Co. was founded.

first vintage Port The 1790 Sandeman shipped by George Sandeman in 1791.

first Chardonnay label The 1936 Pinot Chardonnay from Livermore, California, produced by Ernest Wente was the earliest. Ironically, it was later discovered that Chardonnay was not a Pinot. As late as 1960 there were only 90 hectares (230 acres) of Chardonnay in California; at the beginning of 1995 this had increased to more than 24,400 hectares (62,000 acres).

first wine saver pump In 1985 the Dutch brothers Bernd and John Schneider created the first prototype of Vacu-Vin. Their aim was to prevent part-consumed wine spoiling quickly and the new pump was launched in 1986. A professor of economics recommended that an initial quantity of 20,000 units should be manufactured. One year later the brothers had sold more than one million pumps and just over five years later the figure exceeded ten million. The Vacu-Vin wine saver was the first major invention to help consumers since the corkscrew.

first individual wine chiller In 1992 Bernd and John Schneider launched their second wine accessory. Called Rapid Ice, it is a simple silver sleeve which remains pliable when left in a freezer. Placed over a bottle of wine it chills it in five minutes.

Oldest

oldest French wine brotherhood The French make promotional use of their brotherhoods some of which admit many new members every year. The oldest and most exclusive is Le Confrérie des Chevaliers du Sacavin, which takes its inspiration from the poet Rabelais. It was founded in 1904 at Montreuil-Bellay in the Loire Valley and members are officially inducted in acknowledgement of service to Loire wines.

oldest surviving wine bottle The Speyer Wine Museum in Germany's Rheinhessen region contains a largely intact bottle of Roman origin believed to be about 1600 years old.

oldest vines In the late 1950s several rows of Shiraz vines planted in 1828 on the Wyndham Estate in the Hunter Valley of Australia's New South Wales were still contributing grapes to the vineyard's crush. Many vineyardists can show visitors a small number of extremely old vines but proof of age is virtually impossible. The oldest block still producing wine is probably a section of pre-phylloxera Tannat vines at Domaine Laplace at Aydie in the Madiran appellation in south-west France. They are about 140 years old.

oldest recorded existing vineyard The Josephshöfer Vineyard at Graach in the Mosel Valley of Germany, now owned by the Reichsgraf von Kesselstatt estate. It was ceded to the monks of Martinshöfer by Bishop Magnerice of Trier in

AD 596 and remained in their possession for 1193 years before being purchased by a banker called Josef Hain. There may be cases of older continuous viticulture but proof is, as yet, not available.

oldest wine consumed in the twentieth-century In 1986 Jacques Hebrard, general manager and part-owner of the first growth Saint-Émilion, Château Cheval-Blanc, reported that he and the eminent marine biologist Jacques Cousteau had consumed part of the contents of a Roman amphora estimated to be nearly 2000 years old. He described the liquid as having a pinkish colour but still being wine. When asked if he could state its exact age, he replied: 'I do not know – the vintage was not on the bottle.'

oldest wine press still in use Domaine Laroche, the Chablis producer, has restored a giant thirteenth-century press on l'Obédiencerie, its ancient property. The main arm consists of one massive tree and it takes ten fit men to operate it.

oldest operating winery in the New World Research to date establishes the Marques de Aguayo winery at Hacienda el Rosario in Parras, Mexico, as the oldest New World winery still in operation. It was founded in 1593.

oldest fully intact wine bottle This is a Leisten 1631 from Germany owned by a collector in Sydney, Australia. It came from the cellars of the Bavarian Royal family. The *London Evening News* of 21 December 1910 reported that 'it had been in the possession of David Jones & Sons of Streatham High Road London for some years'. It is believed that they purchased it following the death of Mad King Ludwig.

oldest wine still on regular sale In 1878, at the Seppeltsfield winery in the Barossa Valley, Benno Seppelt had the foresight to start the practice of annually laying down its finest Australian Port with the intention of releasing it only when it was 100 years old. Known as Seppelt's Para Liqueur Port, it sells for over £1000 (A$2,000) a bottle.

oldest wine auction Hospices de Beaune, a
charity founded in 1459, possesses nearly 60
hectares (150 acres) of outstanding vineyards in
Burgundy. The wines are sold annually in a historic auction which becomes a major price indica-
tor for that vintage.

Wine Saints

These are a few of the numerous examples.

Saint-Amour A Beaujolais village appellation whose purple young wine, made from Gamay grapes, takes wise commercial advantage of another saint's day, that of Saint Valentine.

Saint Clement A greatly improved Napa Valley winery which is now making some superb Cabernets in an area where the climate also supports oranges and lemons. Saint Clement was a very early bishop and pope. According to legend he was martyred in about AD 100 by being thrown into the sea with an anchor around his neck.

Saint-Émilion This quaint place claims to be France's oldest wine city but it is difficult to see how it can prove to have existed for longer than Narbonne. Its name comes from an eighth-century hermit monk who, legend relates, stopped there on a pilgrimage south to Santiago de Compostela. He was so attracted by the peaceful surroundings that he carved himself a small stone hermitage and decided to stay. Regardless of the oldest-wine-city debate, Saint-Émilion does produce some of the world's finest red wines.

Saint-Estèphe A highly rated village appellation, the largest and most northerly in the Médoc region, it is home to magnificent red wines such as Château Cos d'Estournel and Château Montrose.

Saint-Fiacre One of the best of the Muscadet villages near Nantes, Saint-Fiacre is named after an Irish-born seventh-century saint. Wine lovers should not be discouraged to learn that he is the patron saint of venereal disease. His patronage seems to work – the vines of the Muscadet villages are entirely free from sexually transmitted diseases.

Saint George The legendary patron saint of England and slayer of dragons or Welshmen. His name adorns the label of one of England's more enterprising attempts at wine production in deepest Sussex.

Saint Hallet An amusing Barossa Valley, South Australia, attempt at a fictional saint. To the surprise of some wine experts in Australia, Saint Hallet was not created through the clever promotional skills of Bob 'Sir Lunch-a-lot' McLean, a director of the winery and former public relations mogul. In fact, Bob once conducted three bishops around the property and offered A$1000 to any of their causes if they could prove the existence of such a saint. The name was apparently used in the locality long before the winery was founded and has an unknown German

heritage. This should not detract from Saint Hallet's delicious wines, specifically the Old Block Shiraz.

Saint-Hilaire-Saint-Florent An important village on the left bank of the Loire and home to Saumur Brut producers such as Bouvet-Ladubay, Veuve Amiot and Ackerman. Saint Hilaire, or Hilary, was the first monk-bishop in Gaul, and the village takes its name from its ruined Benedictine abbey which was active until the French Revolution. Saint Florent was a local saint about whom little is known.

Saint Hugo A fine Coonawarra red from Orlando Wyndham, Australia, which was intro-duced in 1983. Saint Hugo is not an authentic saint, but a serious title in memory of the com-pany's late managing director Hugo Gramp. A member of the founding family, he lost his life in an air disaster at Essendon in 1938, along with fellow wine chiefs Tom Hardy of Hardy's and Sidney Hill Smith of Yalumba. Orlando Wyndham must have decided that 'H' was the best initial for saints because it also has a Chardonnay called St Hilary and a Rhine Riesling named St Helga.

Sainte Hune An eighth-century Alsace saint who was dedicated to tending the sick. Saint Hune treated her patients with wine believed to be from her village, nowadays known as Hunawihr. The tiny single estate that bears her name, Clos Sainte Hune from F.E. Trimbach, is arguably the source of Alsace's finest Riesling and one of the world's greatest values in dry white wine.

Saint-Joseph An increasingly successful, mid-to full-bodied red from the northern Rhône Valley, which seldom disappoints if aged for three or more years. Its title comes from a hillside of the same name, dedicated to Christ's earthly father. It was granted appellation status as recently as 1956 and before that experts knew it as 'Mauves', the name of the local village, which they added to its Côtes du Rhône appellation to distinguish it from other wines. The eminent French writer Victor Hugo referred to it as 'this good wine of Mauves' in *Les Miserables*.

Saint-Julien One of the smallest appellations in the Médoc, Saint-Julien is the home of great châteaux like Léoville Lascases, Ducru-Beaucaillou and Gruaud-Larose, which produce outstanding, second growth red Bordeaux. Saint Julien is the patron of innkeepers.

Saint Martin Many believe that Saint Martin truly deserves the title patron saint of wine, but for some unknown reason he has been burdened with quite the opposite – patron saint of drunkards. It is likely that his experience as a junior officer in the Roman army enabled this great Bishop of Tours to have more influence on the early cultivation of vineyards in France than any other person: wherever the Romans settled they planted vineyards and when Martin became Bishop he encouraged his parish priests to follow the same practice.

An apocryphal story about a diocesan visit Martin made one winter to a neighbouring parish is still told in the Loire Valley. On arrival the bishop tethered his donkey to some vines which he believed belonged to the church. When he returned the next morning he was confronted by a furious wine grower who complained that the animal had eaten all the greenery on his plants, and demanded compensation. Without hesitation Martin acquiesced. When he returned 12 months later he was accosted by the same *vigneron* who told him that he had experienced the finest crop ever, and it was all thanks to the donkey – which had, of course, accidentally invented pruning.

Saint Pantaléon or Pantaleimon This Christian martyr, who died in about AD 305, is claimed by both a full-bodied red Côtes du Rhône and a sweet white Cyprus blend. Saint Pantaléon was a doctor whose name translates as 'all-compassionate'. It is possible that he used wine as a medicine.

Saint Raphael In the 1840s the French chemist Alphonse Jamet caused irreparable damage to his eyesight by toiling in his laboratory night after night in dim candlelight. His task was to produce the recipe for a wine-based aperitif in which quinine could be dissolved, to enable French soldiers serving in North Africa to take this protection against malaria in a form which masked the bitter taste of the drug. Jamet was beaten in the race by Joseph Dubonnet, but still made a notable contribution to the needs of the French army. As his eyesight faded he asked Saint Raphael the archangel (also a patron saint of healing) to give him sufficient sight to complete his task. When his prayers were answered he promised to give thanks by naming his new drink Saint Raphael.

Saint Vincent The patron saint of wine producers, his feast on 22 January is celebrated with
fêtes and competitions, especially in the
Beaujolais and Burgundy regions. The legend is
that in heaven Saint Vincent became so desperate
for a glass of fine French wine that he sought
permission to return to earth again so that he
might enjoy that pleasure once more.

Santa Margherita Major Italian producer from
the Veneto. It is famed for being the first to sell

Pinot Grigio which was discovered by chance on a small mountain farm. The wine proved so successful that Santa Margherita now blend and market it from numerous growers throughout the Alto Adige. Santa Margherita was a thirteenth-century farmer's daughter who undertook a life of self-denial, austerity and penance in remorse for an earlier period of dubious morality. Her incorrupt body survives in Cortona.

San Patricio One of the most elegant of all Fino Sherries, San Patricio is made by Garvey and is also the name of its famous cathedral-like bodega which is over 150 metres (500 feet) long. The house was founded in 1780 by William Garvey, an Irish horse breeder, who named both his son and his great bodega after the patron saint of his homeland: Saint Patrick.

Santa Rita This major winery, founded in the Maipo valley of Chile in 1880, makes attractive wines at all levels. It has some of the finest vineyard slopes in the country and Casa Real, its top-of-the-range Cabernet, is a memorable bottle. It was named after the patron saint of desperate cases.

Intriguing Stories

Bouvet-Ladubay This sparkling Saumur house now owned by Champagne Taittinger, was founded by Etienne Bouvet in 1851. Local legend suggests that the business struggled until the 1880s when the Bouvet family discovered a vast hoard of jewels that the monks of Saint-Hilaire-Saint-Florent had abandoned in their *tuffeau* caves when they fled during the French Revolution. (*Tuffeau* is the name given to the soft, chalky limestone of the central Loire Valley.) The Bouvet family suddenly built new houses, sent their children to be educated privately in England, took regular holidays on the French Riviera and adopted many other trappings of wealth.

The matter is unlikely ever to be proven but strong circumstantial evidence has survived through a local newspaper, *La Petite Loire* which in 1892 published this report by a journalist named Manoury: 'According to some they [the Bouvet family] had dug out gold coins then ten gold crosses and even gold crosses of St Hilaire and St Florent.' In addition, a handwritten poem by a disgruntled former employee, which came to light in 1971, gives a detailed account of the discovery of seven barrels and of the different jewels found in each one. Finally, while the house of Bouvet-Ladubay has never officially admitted anything, their prestige Saumur Brut is named 'Sapphir'.

the case of the cellar master's murder Agatha Christie fans would have been disappointed at the challenge set by the murder of Robert Billion in April 1984, for the perpetrator, his wife, confessed her guilt without a moment's hesitation. After years of desperation her patience had snapped and she had stabbed her 62-year-old husband so violently with a pair of kitchen scissors that he slumped to his death.

The unusual factor was that Robert Billion was an important cellar master: the man responsible for the production of the smallest of all the Grandes Marques Champagnes and the most exclusive of all the houses, the unique Salon le Mesnil. He was just beginning to prepare for his 35th vintage in charge when, it was reported, he over-indulged in his two favourite recreations. He enjoyed drinking Champagne – understandably – but he was also a notorious philanderer. Time and again his relations with his long-suffering wife had been jeopardised and, finally, he had pushed her one step too far.

The French court, understandably sympathetic to Madame Billion, decided that hers was a true *crime de passion* and ordered her immediate release.

Early in 1996 Salon, the perfectionist among Champagne houses, was still shipping only its 1982 and 1983 vintages, the youngest it was prepared to release. Both were made by a man who had already been dead for 12 years.

Château Mouton-Rothschild In 1924 Baron Philippe de Rothschild commissioned an artist, Jean Carlu, to decorate the label of his great château. The practice became established in 1945 and since then a string of renowned names,

including Salvadore Dali, Jean Cocteau, Marc Chagall and Henry Moore have seen their work displayed on successive vintages. They have always been paid in kind.

However, the baron was not always delighted. In 1986 his general manager, Philippe Cottin, revealed that a number of rejected label paintings by celebrated artists had never been used and remained locked away in secret at the château.

Château Smith-Haut-Lafitte In 1720 George Smith, a successful Scottish-born wine *negoçiant* with cellars on the Quai des Chartrons in

Bordeaux, decided to invest in a wine château and bought a fine vineyard near Martillac in the Graves region. There he built himself an imposing property which became home to his wife and two sons.

Unfortunately George fell in love with a beautiful peasant girl, Elizabeth Louis, and shocked his contemporaries by living with his mistress. He was castigated by the Bordeaux court of morals who ordered him to return to his wife and family or be ostracised by his fellows. George refused to mend his ways and was never able to trade on the Chartrons again.

Est! Est!! Est!!! Six exclamation marks seem an exaggeration for this fairly ordinary, dry white wine from the Lazio province of Italy but their existence may be more than coincidental with the wine region's alleged date of origin. In AD 1111 Johann Fugger, the wine-loving Bishop of Augsburg in Bavaria, was travelling from his diocese to Rome for the coronation of the Holy Roman Emperor Henry V. He preferred to select his overnight accommodation according to the quality of its wine and each day would send his valet Martin ahead with instructions to chalk the word 'est' on the door of any suitable hostelry. When the bishop reached the town of Montefiascone, just one day's ride from Rome, he found to his delight the words 'Est! Est!! Est!!!' on the door of an inn. Legend relates that he failed to arrive at the coronation.

Goldfield wine When André Heriard-Dubreuil, the Chairman of Remy Cognac, decided in the 1960s that the company should start producing brandy and wine in Australia, he used an extremely original method to select a suitable site for a vineyard. He took two maps of Australia, one of the cool weather areas and the other of existing and abandoned goldfield locations. At the time, some Australian vineyards were planted in areas with excessively high temperatures that resulted in dull, flabby wines but Dubreuil realised that the combination of a cool climate and the alluvial soils found in many goldfields would be ideal for grapes, as they would help give freshness and acidity. So he placed one map over the other revealing just two places that matched. One, in Western Australia, was too far away for their needs and the other was located at Avoca in the Blue Pyrenees of Victoria. There he found a small, deep lake which was a flooded gold mine, sheltered by hills on three sides. It fulfilled all his requirements and became known as the Blue Pyrenees Estate.

'The answer lies in the soil!' Bob Rowan, a London solicitor, is a Burgundy fanatic – to the extent that he has collected soil samples from 144 Grand Cru vineyards which he keeps in jam jars. He takes great delight in serving his guests the finest Burgundies with the corresponding soil sample alongside.

Khan Krum This popular Bulgarian Chardonnay takes its name from an ancient legend. When the country was under Ottoman control the Muslim leader, Khan Krum, ordered the destruction of all vineyards. One night one of his lions escaped from its cage and caused widespread panic until a courageous youth called Mavrud slew the beast with his bare hands.

Khan Krum immediately announced that he would reward Mavrud's bravery, but insisted on learning the secret of his strength. When the youth's trembling mother told him she had kept one vine and used its grapes to make wine – and that this had given her son his power – Khan Krum repealed his law and vineyards were planted again throughout the land. The surviving variety of vine was given the name Mavrud, a name which it still bears today.

Napoleon and the Madeira he never drank When HMS *Northumberland* took Napoleon Bonaparte to exile on St Helena it made a brief stop at the island of Madeira. The defeated emperor, who was something of a wine lover, requested, and was granted, permission to buy a pipe of Cossart 1793 Vintage Madeira which was hauled on board for the long journey. Sadly, when Napoleon reached St Helena he was suffering from serious stomach problems and his doctor ordered total abstinence. After his death the untouched cask was returned to Madeira where it was bought by John Blandy and blended with other vintages in order to be sold as a 1793 Blandy solera – which seems tough on Cossart who made the original wine.

Presbyterian wine Many may think of Presbyterians as synonymous with total abstinence but occasionally that is not true. In 1978, St David's Presbyterian Church in the vineyard town of Mudgee, New South Wales, decided that wine could boost its image and so made 500 cases of red wine and 500 of white which were labelled with the church's name to celebrate its centenary.

Is this an unique case of a non-conformist church having its own label wine?

Pyramid 1 In an experiment in 1982 the Almaden Wine Company in San José, California, aged various wines under a hanging pyramid in the belief that this would improve their quality. The wines were packed into cardboard cases for shipping and placed under the pyramid until required. No reports of any outstanding successes were ever reported.

Pyramid 2 In 1986 Alfred Tesseron, a director of three Bordeaux châteaux – Pontet-Canet, Lafon-Rochet and Malescasse – launched an experiment for ageing wine in the Courbu pyramid, an exact reproduction of the Cheops one.

Taylor 1927 Vintage Port There is a story that some may consider apocryphal but others insist is true, concerning an elderly lady who in the late

1970s was a regular customer of a fine wine shop in London's South Kensington. Every five or six weeks she would buy a bottle of what some experts claim is the finest example of vintage Port ever drunk. She returned to the shop year after year, seeking her highly prized trophy, and all its staff considered her a dedicated wine buff. Then one day the inevitable happened. She was told that the last Taylor '27 had been sold but that she need not worry because the 1935 was excellent. She was utterly distraught. How could her house plants possibly survive without their regular helping of Taylor '27 sediment she asked – while at the same time remarking that the Port itself was of no real interest for she always poured it down the drain.

the Port-drinking bulldog Trespassers near Gelorup in Western Australia should take care not to stray on to the property of Leschenault, run by Dr Barry Killerby. For, according to Australian wine guru James Halliday, it is the home of a Port-drinking British bulldog called Jackson.

However Dr Killerby, a man with a most inviting name, does not produce Port and one is left with the image of a British bulldog slurping his bowlful of Taylor '55 or Graham's '63.

64

top of the ladder In the 1980s the keeper of one of the bodegas at the famous Sherry house of Gonzales Byass noticed a mouse nibbling the crumbs that fell from his sandwich. Being a lover of animals, he offered it a sip from his lunch-time glass of Sherry. The mouse appeared to enjoy this and a daily routine began whereby it and a few relatives would arrive for midday refreshment. The bodega-keeper even built a tiny set of stairs enabling the mice to reach the lip of the glass more readily and help themselves to the Sherry.

The event gradually became a talking-point and for several years visitors insisted on witnessing the spectacle. But the inevitable happened. A cat arrived and the lunch menu changed abruptly!

In Vino Veritas

A heavy drinker was offered grapes at dessert.
'No thank you,' he said, pushing the dish away
from him. 'I am not in the habit of taking my
wine in the form of pills.'
Brillat-Savarin (1755–1826), La Physiologie du Goût

Stop drinking nothing but water; take a little
wine for the sake of your digestion, for your fre-
quent ailments.
St Paul writing to Timothy, 1 Timothy 5, 23

Wine is the best liquor to wash glasses in.
Jonathan Swift (1667–1745)

The alcohol in wine is as the canvas upon which
an artist paints a picture.
André Simon (1877–1970)

Old newsreels of John F. Kennedy's memorable
'Ich bin ein Berliner' speech in June 1963 show
initial bemusement on the faces of many specta-
tors. For as Hamburg is to the hamburger and
Frankfurt to the frankfurter, so Berlin is to a
berliner and the United States President had identified himself as a doughnut. Perhaps he was
inspired by the generous volumes of wine enjoyed
at the lunch-time reception, given by Berlin's
mayor Willy Brandt, which had included a superb
1961 Reichsgraf von Kesselstatt Piesporter
Grafenberg.

If God forbade drinking, would He have made
wine so good?
Cardinal Richelieu (1585–1642)

Here with a loaf of bread beneath the bough,
a flask of wine, a book of verse – and thou
beside me singing in the wilderness –
and wilderness is Paradise enow.
Omar Khayyam (eleventh century), The Rubaiyat

Wine is bottled poetry.
Robert Louis Stevenson (1850–94)

There are . . . more old drunkards than old physicians.
Rabelais (1495–1553), Gargantua

Wine can be considered with good reason as the most healthful and the most hygienic of all beverages.
Louis Pasteur (1822–95)

Sir Winston Churchill usually drank Champagne for breakfast and explained to Odette Pol Roger the reasons for his change from full-size bottles to imperial pints: 'When I drink from a bottle I'm happy, when I drink from a half-bottle I'm not happy but Clementine is happy, but to make us both happy I will drink imperial pints.'

Referring to reports in 1875 that the 3rd marquess of Bute was attempting to revive British viti-culture by producing wine from a vineyard at Castell Coch near Cardiff, *Punch* magazine commented: 'If the wine is ever made, it will take four to drink it, two to hold the victim down and one to pour it down his throat.'

Vinum regum, rex vinorum (the wine of kings and the king of wines). Voltaire (1694–1778), writing to Louis XIV of France about the qualities of the Hungarian dessert wine Tokay Essencia. The phrase was later borrowed by the makers of Champagne. Voltaire may well have heard it used in Vienna where the Austrian wine Gumpoldskirchen had been using the accolade for centuries.

Voltaire also wrote of Tokay Essencia: 'It contains such strength and sweetness that it renews one's vital energy. It brings new life to each brain cell and lights a firework of bliss in the depth of the soul.'

Label Awards

the least inspired label Kanga Rouge, an Australian wine that hopped into the UK market in 1980. There were two versions: the first came from the Rothbury Estate in the Hunter Valley and the second from Coonawarra. The original wine was destined for France but it was denied entry because it bore the word 'Hermitage', which in France is only permitted for wines from that region. An emergency label change is said to have inspired *Decanter* magazine's 'Worst Wine Label' feature.

the naughtiest label Cuvée Sexy Côtes du Rhone J-M Saut Negoçiant Codolet from the mid-1980s displayed a bare-bottomed model posing in a rather uncomfortable position. Its sales did not set any records.

the beefiest label This title must go to the late 1980s' label Aberdeen-Angus Cabernet Sauvignon which displayed a large bull. It came from a producer called Govenechea in Mendoza, Argentina.

the least tempting label Herpe's La Clape VDQS wins this award. It comes from Paul Herpe et Fils, wine producers within the VDQS appellation of La Clape in the Languedoc Roussillon region of France. No professional tasting notes describing it could be found.

the most corny label Bow-Jlay Noove-Oh 1985 from the Caves du Val de Saône.

the most smuggled label Le Brick, a French vin de table label sold in Madame Morand's grocery store in St Malo, caused quite a few tourist chuckles in the 1980s. Some Portsmouth and Plymouth customs officers soon became aware of high-spirited travellers declaring that they only had a few bricks.

the most honest label award This must go to Cheap Red Wine, a blended Californian wine from the humbly named Vin Ordinaire Ltd of Gilroy.

the most unlikely label Policia Vinho Branco from Violanta Matias Miranda of Lisbon depicts a policeman standing to attention.

the most awful franglais label Nuits Sans Merde Specially labelled en Engleterre par le Permission des Prime Minister ey le Minister d'Environment Grandvin du Whale 1981 Coté de Solihull sur Blythe Pecheur, Palmier, Brun et Balseche (*Reproduced with the kind permission of* Decanter *magazine*)

the wine imbiber's label Booser Paradiesgarden Riesling Graf A Franz Von Spee'schke from Germany's Nahe Valley.

the crudest label Pisse Vieille Brouilly, Georges Duboeuf, tied with Cat's Pee on a Gooseberry Bush, Gisborne Sauvignon Blanc, New Zealand 1995. The latter is said by its makers to taste somewhat better than the name but how do they know?

the most amorous label Passionwine, a
Pokolbin Cellars label from the Hunter Valley, New
South Wales, depicting naked couples.

**the most awkward to pronounce label (and
probably one of the longest)** Staatliche
Weinbaudomäne Schlossböckelheimer
Kupfergrube Riesling Kabinett 1994, Nahe.

Great Wine Disasters

Austrian wine scandal In July 1985 all Austrian wines were withdrawn from export markets after traces of an anti-freeze agent, diethylene-glycol, a substance also used in air-conditioning equipment, were found in samples. Some unscrupulous producers had developed a method of using it to mask the illegal addition of sugar to their wines. This enabled them, for example, to raise sweet wines from the category of Spätlese to Beerenauslese, and thus substantially increased their profits.

The scandal naturally gave rise to corny jokes about filling the car radiator with Austrian wine. More seriously, certain businesses went into liquidation and the guilty parties were imprisoned.

Fortunately, no one was taken seriously ill but the fraud wreaked havoc on Austrian wines which were banned from export trade for four years. Export was only resumed after the introduction of drastic new wine laws. Ironically, Austria can today claim some of the greatest sweet white wines.

the battle of Castillon 1453 should be firmly engrained on the brains, if not the palates, of all British lovers of red Bordeaux or Claret. It was the year in which the British under John Talbot, the 1st Earl of Shrewsbury, lost the battle of Castillon and with it the ownership of Aquitaine including the vineyards of Bordeaux. It is all the more puzzling that Château Talbot, named after the ill-fated earl, should be a favourite wine of Elizabeth II.

Italian wine scandal In 1986 several people died in northern Italy after drinking cheap wines fortified with industrial alcohol. The story was reported all over the world but because it was a domestic concern reaction was limited and Italian wine fortunately continued its export sales without a hitch.

Jefferson's Champagne On 1 December 1803 the United States President, Thomas Jefferson, recorded in his cellar book that 153 bottles of champagne out of a consignment of 400 from Ay had broken. Strangely, these were not sparkling Champagne, for Jefferson preferred to purchase the still version, known as 'Tranquil'. This suggests that, after travelling, a secondary fermentation had started which built up pressure and burst the bottles.

Phylloxera This vine disease, spread by the aphid *phylloxera vastatrix*, causes vine roots to wither, preventing the absorption of water which, in turn, results in the death of the plant. The true facts concerning the damage caused by the aphid in western Europe during the late nineteenth and early twentieth centuries will never be known as its threatened path may have caused unnecessary panic. Wine growers often grubbed out vineyards and abandoned land when the louse was still many miles away.

Phylloxera had always existed on the eastern seaboard of the United States and is believed to have crossed to Europe when vine cuttings were shipped from America to a greenhouse at Hammersmith, London, in the 1850s. It was first identified in France in 1860. It swept through virtually all the French wine regions and other wine-producing countries of the world as they imported affected cuttings. Only Chile remains free of the disease because of its sandy soils and isolated location. In France in the 1870s it was considered by many to be a greater disaster than the country's defeat in the Franco-Prussian War.

It remains a threat in many countries although in the nineteenth century it was discovered that grafting European cuttings on to resistant American rootstock was the answer (see 'Colourful Characters': **Munson, Thomas**). Ironically, many of the world's wine regions still risk using ungrafted vines because of the expense involved.

Prohibition The United States' ban on alcohol came into force on 16 January 1920 and was repealed on 5 December 1933. The law, called the Volstead Act was sponsored by Congressman Andrew Volstead from Yellow Medicine County, Minnesota, and caused America to lose at least two generations of wine drinkers. Although home-made wine-making was permitted, the development of professional standards was halted and commercial wines were unavailable. With the economic distress of the 1930s and the Second World War, it wasn't until the 1960s that the country's wine industry began to revive.

Teheran cellar destruction When the last Shah of Persia left the Peacock throne in 1979 and brought the Pahlavi dynasty to an end, he also abandoned a wine cellar of immense value. Within days, supporters of the Ayatollah Khomeini had forced entry into it and started the systematic destruction of its contents, which included large quantities of Champagne and other fine French wines worth hundreds of thousands of pounds.

Barrels and Bottles

BARRELS

Sizes are always approximate because each is individually coopered by hand. In Europe barrels have traditionally been made from oak or, in the past, chestnut, while in California some giant redwood storage vats were used in the 1960s and 1970s but many have been replaced.

barrique 225 litre (49½ gallon) cask best known in Bordeaux but widely seen throughout the rest of France and in the New World. It is used primarily for the ageing of red wines. New or young *barriques* impart oak tannins while allowing new wine to breathe. Called *a pièce* in Burgundy.

botti General Italian term for 'barrel', often used to describe large casks of 1000 or more litres (220-plus gallons).

butt Origninally an English cask that contained ale. It was later used for Madeira, Sherry or Malaga. Its capacity is normally approximately 500–600 litres (110–132 gallons).

Dubonnet cask This historic barrel is still on display in the Dubonnet cellars at Thuir in the foothills of the French Pyrenees. In the middle of the nineteenth century it was said to be the world's largest cask and was seen by hundreds of thousands, if not millions, of visitors. However, it could have fitted within the Heidelberg Tun (see below) with plenty of room to spare.

foudre or fuder A large barrel used in Alsace and Germany for the ageing of wine. Old oak casks do not add tannin but the pores permit the wine to breathe. These casks generally have a capacity of about 1000 litres (220 gallons) and many are over 100 years old.

fut A generic French term for a barrel or large cask.

Halbstück Barrel with capacity of about 650 litres (143 gallons) in which wines are aged in the Rheingau region of Germany.

Heidelberg tun Possibly the largest of all barrels, it has a capacity of 220,000 litres (48,400 gallons) and was coopered for the Elector Karl Theodor in 1751. The vessel still stands in Heidelberg Castle. Its career can hardly claim to have been success-ful: in 2½ centuries it has been full on only three occasions and has for generations suffered a leak which defies repair.

hogshead A relatively small cask which varies slightly in size depending upon the region in which it is used. In Burgundy it is usually about 225 litres (49½ gallons) but in Portugal often about 250–260 litres (55–57 gallons).

octave A little cask which has proved particularly practical in narrow cellars or ones where space is limited. The octave is used in the production of small volumes of an individual wine from one parcel of vines. It varies in size from 70–80 litres (15½–17½ gallons) and is easily handled by one person.

pipe A fairly large tapered cask of English origin, used for ageing and storing fortified wines. Most widely found in the Port lodges, it is also popular in Madeira and Marsala. Volumes vary considerably with approximate sizes being: Oporto 520–550 litres (114½–121 gallons), Madeira 400–420 litres (88–92½ gallons) and Marsala 420–430 litres (92½–94½ gallons).

tonneau Best known as a 900 litre (198 gallon) barrel for Bordeaux wines, it represents 100 cases of wine. Its measurement has been a unit of trade in the wholesale markets for generations.

BOTTLES

bocksbeutel An eighteenth-century flat flask from Franconia in Germany and Styria in Austria, which is still popular in these regions though rarely seen in the export markets. Its design is said to be copied from a goat's scrotum.

bouteille Bottle, of which there are over 50 known shapes and sizes in France alone.

fassle A German wine vessel, sometimes made of leather, from which the contents are squirted into the mouth. Now used only at festivals and other celebrations.

flagon A wine flagon is usually made of green glass unlike the better-known brown ones for beer or cider. It is a large, flattish bottle often used in New World countries to hold inexpensive wines.

fiasco Many wine guides simply describe the *fiasco* as an Italian bottle or flask, sometimes contained in a straw basket. But there is more to it than that. When the Etruscans began to develop glass production in the fourth century BC they discovered that it was possible to blow a bottle in the shape of a round bubble. However, when the bubble cooled and they tried to stand it upright it fell over – it was a *fiasco*, a failure. To correct the problem they asked their women to weave flat straw bases into which the bottle was inserted. The *fiasco* can still be seen in Chianti and Orvieto.

fillette A slim half-bottle which is still widely found in the Loire Valley.

flute d'Alsace A tall, slender bottle used for Alsace wine.

jug A large bottle with a handle. It measures one US gallon and usually contains pasteurised wine of a basic quality, a favourite purchase of President Clinton when he was governor of Arkansas.

porrón A Spanish flask with an extended neck, or spout, often made of kid leather or wood. It is popular in the Basque region and regularly seen on sporting occasions when it facilitates the swift consumption of wine.

pot Also known as *le pot de Beaujolais*, this is a half-litre, gently curved bottle still found in restaurants. Piat, the prominent Beaujolais *negoçiants*, have their own 75 centilitre (cl) version.

Sizes of bottles

Bordeaux sizes
150cl: Magnum
225cl: Marie-Jeanne
300cl: Double magnum
450cl: Jeroboam
600cl: *Impériale*

Burgundy sizes
150cl: Magnum
300cl: Jeroboam
450cl: Rehoboam
600cl: Methuselah

Champagne sizes
20cl: A split or quarter.

37.5cl: A half-bottle.

55cl: A medium or pint bottle (no longer made but some examples survive).

75cl: A bottle.

1.5 litres/2 bottles: Magnum.

3 litres/4 bottles: Jeroboam (a son of Solomon and King of Israel c. 922–c. 901 BC).

4.5 litres/6 bottles: Rehoboam (also a son of Solomon and King of the divided land of Judah c. 922–c. 915 BC). No longer produced because of European Union legislation which insists on sizes in full litres.

6 litres/8 bottles: Methuselah (the oldest person in the Bible, accredited with 969 years in Genesis 5).

9 litres/12 bottles: Salmanazar (an eighth-century King of Assyria, 2 Kings 17).

12 litres/16 bottles: Balthazar (son of Nebuchadnezzar and a sixth-century BC King of Babylon, famous for his feast and the writing on the wall.)

15 litres/20 bottles: Nebuchadnezzar (King of Babylon 604–561 BC). He enslaved the Hebrews – and also created the Hanging Gardens of Babylon, one of the seven wonders of the ancient world.

Quite how these bottle names were introduced is not known, other than that they were found in Great Britain from the first half of the nineteenth century.

tappit hen An ancient vessel, believed to be of Scottish origin, used for wine or liquor. Before the eighteenth century it was available as one, three or six quarts but in the nineteenth and early twentieth centuries it was used mainly for Port and was 2½ times the normal bottle size. The tappit hen is no longer made but is occasionally seen in auctions.

Vines

There are 26 species of vine of which one, *Vitis vinifera*, dominates wine production. It has over 5000 different varieties according to the University of California/Sotheby *Book of California Wine* and, in world terms, about 30 of these are used in the production of good quality wines.

hybrid vines Crossings of two different varieties, often developed to cope with difficult climatic conditions.

the most prolific wild vines These are found in the High Plains of Texas, home to 14 of the world's 26 vine species.

most original use of vines Some growers in the Western Cape of South Africa plant Pontac, a red-skinned grape with red flesh. The vines are usually restricted to a few rows next to the mountainside, to fool the baboons who, during the dry season, wander down in search of refreshment. When they pick the Pontac grapes they see the red juice on their hands and, fearing that it is blood, flee back to the mountains.

promiscuous growth In some parts of Italy, particularly the Chianti region of Tuscany, an ancient system of land-sharing called 'promiscuous growth' is still in evidence. It involves a vineyard owner permitting his workers to plant fruit and vegetables in the spaces between the vine stocks. One can stumble across bush tomatoes, cabbages and onions, their colours adding variety to the

landscape. Could this practice have been the origin of the vegetal nose that some writers describe a wine as having?

red, white and pink grapes Red and rosé wines are normally made from red grapes, although some sparkling rosé is made by mixing red and white wines. White grapes produce white wine. One curious exception is the grapes on Gewürztraminer vines which are a mix of pink and yellow. The resultant wine can be one of the deepest in colour for a white.

searching for suitable soil Viticulturists employed by Jamieson's Run in South Australia use natural tracking methods when searching for a narrow strip of red soil suitable for red wine vineyards at Coppermura to the north of

Coonawarra in South Australia. With existing *terra rossa* (red soil) plantings reaching extraordinary prices they have been prospecting for potential new sites. This is done by chasing sheep during the dusty summer season to see if any of their wool is a rusty red colour.

Main White Grape Varieties

Aligoté This produces acidic dry white wine and is found principally in Burgundy. For many years it was seen as a swilling white for consumption when young, while finer white Burgundies from Chardonnay grapes were allowed to age. But in the last generation, growers in the village of Bouzeron have developed an individual appellation that specialises in Aligoté and have enhanced its reputation.

Chardonnay Currently the most popular white noble variety in the world. For centuries it has produced white Burgundies like Chablis and Puligny-Montrachet but in the 1970s, in California in particular, it began to show that it is a much more versatile grape than the Burgundians have always claimed. Its wines vary from almost medium-dry un-oaked styles, ideal for immediate consumption, to elegant, dry, barrel-aged examples. More recently, Australians have been especially successful with their leading brands – Jacob's Creek, Hardy's, Lindemans, Penfold's, Preece and Wolf Blass all market popular examples – as has New Zealand with Cook's, Babich, Kumeu River, Stoneleigh and the mighty Cloudy Bay. Another exciting source is America's Washington State where l'Ecole 41, Hogue Cellars and Arbor Crest are making consistently good wines.

Chenin Blanc One of the most versatile yet mis-understood varieties. It is a fine grape for long ageing, but most of its wines are drunk in their infancy and hence unappreciated. At Saumur in France it is pressed for sparkling wine, at Savennières for fine dry white and in Bonnezeaux for sweet wines of great ageing potential. In California it regularly disappoints in inexpensive medium-dry blends. It shows considerable poten-tial in parts of South Africa but is probably at its peak in Western Australia where labels such as Peel Estate and Moondah Brook produce superb, dry, full-bodied, oak-aged wines.

Gewürztraminer This is widely translated as the 'spicy traminer' because it yields a powerfully aro-matic wine. The variety has caught the imagina-tion of viticulturists around the world but Alsace still remains the home of classic dry 'Gewurtz' with Trimbach Seigneurs de Ribeaupierre and Léon Beyer Comtes d'Eguisheim the most widely acknowledged *cuvées*. In Germany it sells as everyday medium-dry blended wine but in the Napa Valley in California Joseph Phelps lists a dis-tinctive medium-sweet style, and both Columbia and Staton Hills in Washington State are strong contenders.

Grüner Veltliner This fruity, fresh, dry white is Austria's most successful varietal and supplies about one-third of the total wine volume. There are further plantings in limited quantities in other countries in Eastern Europe.

Melon Bourgogne A Muscadet grape, so-named because of its melon-shaped leaves. It was first brought to Brittany from Burgundy and planted at Château de Cassemichère in 1709 after a disastrous winter that destroyed all the region's red vines. Its bone dry but mildly fruity wine is ideal with seafood. Among the top-rated names are Domaine de Chasseloire, Château du Cleray and Louis Metereau.

Muscat Blanc à Petits Grains This has an abundance of synonyms including Muscat de Frontignan, Muscat d'Alsace, Moscato di Canelli, Brown Muscat (Australia), Moscatel Dorado (Spain), Muscatel Branco (Portugal) and Muskadel (South Africa). It first achieved recognition as Muscat of Samos. In recent years the variety has been responsible for the popularisation of Muscat de Beaumes de Venise. As Moscato di Canelli its most notable success has been achieved with Asti. In Alsace, Muscat is usually vinified as a dry white, but other variations of the grape are also found there including Muscat Ottonel.

Palomino The most important grape of Spain's Sherry region, responsible for about 90 per cent of the plantings. In its pure form it gives a dry white wine. It is also planted in Australia, California and South Africa and there are small quantities in southern France and Portugal.

Pinot Blanc/Pinot Bianco Once used for Champagne, it gives its best results as a clean, fresh, lightly fruity wine in Alsace.

Pinot Gris/Pinot Grigio/Ruländer Arguably one of the most under-rated varieties, it produces fine, firm, full-bodied wines in Alsace with excellent examples from Trimbach, Hugel, Jos Meyer and many others. In New Zealand the tiny Dry River winery at Martinborough has an outstanding Pinot Gris, as does Adelsheim in Oregon.

Riesling At its best its wines are among the finest in the world. Two Trimbach wines from Alsace, Clos Sainte-Hune and Cuvée Frédéric-Émile, are perhaps the greatest dry examples and Schloss Johnnisberg in Germany's Rheingau offers outstanding sweet examples. Both styles age extremely well. Riesling produces many other fine dry wines in Alsace and attractive medium-dry and sweet wines in Germany. Also known as the Rhine, Johannisberg or White Riesling, it generally produces less distinctive but good value wines in Australia, New Zealand, South Africa and California.

Sauvignon Blanc Best suited to cool climates such as New Zealand where it appears to have found its paradise with superb examples like Cloudy Bay, Villa Maria, Stoneleigh, Babich, Limeburner's Bay, Matua Valley, Nobilo and the remarkably good value Cook's. In France it excels with Pouilly-Fumé, Sancerre and Quincy. American Sauvignon Blanc tends to have more residual sugar.

Sémillon For many years identified as a main component of Graves Blanc and Sauternes, it occupies more than two-thirds of the vineyards of the greatest Sauternes, Château d'Yquem. More recently it has achieved widespread success in Australia where McWilliam's Elizabeth label from the Hunter Valley is a classic dry version and Brown Brothers and Lindeman's botrytised

Sémillon (see 'Winespeak': **Noble Rot**) are excellent late-picked examples.

Viognier Once restricted to the tiny appellations of Condrieu and Château-Grillet in the northern Rhône Valley, its magnificent mouth-filling dry white wines are best consumed at 18–24 months. Viognier has now spread across France and the New World. It is also used occasionally in the blend of its red neighbour, the illustrious Côte Rôtie.

Main Red Grape Varieties

Cabernet Franc Until the late 1970s Cabernet Franc was more widely found in France than Cabernet Sauvignon. It produces world-class wine at Château Cheval-Blanc in Saint-Émilion and blends well with Merlot in many other wines from that appellation. It is probably at its most characteristic in good vintages of Chinon, Bourgueil and Saint-Nicolas de Bourgueil in the Loire. So far it has not been especially successful as a varietal in the New World but time will tell.

Cabernet Sauvignon This classic red Bordeaux variety has become the role model for the world's winemakers and yet its wines are too dry and austere for millions of consumers. It is at its finest in the great Bordeaux châteaux like Lafite, Latour, Margaux and Mouton-Rothschild. Other exceptional examples are: Caymus Cellars Special Selection and Joe Heitz Martha's Vineyard in Napa Valley, California; Leonetti Cellar in Washington State; and Parker Estate in Coonawarra, Australia.

Cabernet Sauvignon provides superb value in Chile, where outstanding results should be obtained around the year 2005 from recent plantings in the foothills of the Andes, particularly in the Maipo Valley. It has tremendous potential in parts of Argentina, and in Bulgaria where great strides may surprise competitors earlier than expected. In South Africa a new generation of winemakers will surely succeed very soon if they can ignore half the oak purchased by previous generations. Indeed, almost every wine-producing country has some Cabernet Sauvignon, a variety that loves warm sunshine.

Gamay This grape monopolises the Beaujolais region where it is the source of large volumes of popular wine. It can make really good wines in some villages but so far has never produced anything that experts call great. Fleurie, Morgon and Moulin-à-Vent are some of the most attractive examples.

Grenache (Garnacha) It is fair to call Grenache the ubiquitous red. Its greatest achievement is Château Rayas, for many the giant in

Châteauneuf-du-Pape. Its Tavel Rosé delights those who love flavour and it is also an ideal variety for blending, particularly in southern France and northern Spain.

Merlot This is best known for its results in the Pomerol district of Bordeaux, namely Château Petrus and Château La Fleur-Petrus and other magnificent wines in that appellation, as well as in Saint-Émilion. Other excellent examples are: Newton Vineyards and Sterling Vineyards in the Napa Valley, California; The Hogue Cellars and Leonetti Cellar in Washington State; and Backsberg and Fairview in Paarl, South Africa.

In Chile an increasing volume of attractive inexpensive and mid-priced examples are available and some stunning top-level wines will be found there fairly soon. Santa Rita's Reserve Merlot is an ideal flag-bearer.

Pinotage South Africa's own variety which comes from a crossing in 1927 of the Pinot Noir and Cinsault. Kanonkop makes a delicious, full-bodied and beautifully balanced example. Uiterwyk, Simonsig and the curiously named Woolworth's Reserve are not far behind.

Pinot Meunier This is an unfamiliar name to many. Best known in the Champagne region, it gives body and character.

Pinot Noir The red grape that many growers find the most challenging. If any variety could be called temperamental Pinot Noir is it. At its finest in the Burgundy region it produces some of the world's greatest reds like Romanée-Conti and Chambertin. It is attracting worldwide acclaim in Oregon but has disappointed in many other New World locations. Clearly it loves warm weather with some cool relief and dislikes heat that is too intense. The Yarra Valley in Victoria, Australia, the Anderson Valley in California and the Casablanca Valley in Chile may yet prove to be consistent and plentiful sources of well-balanced Pinot Noir.

Sangiovese The strident red vine of Tuscany is scattered throughout central Italy. It is the principal grape for Chianti and the world-class Brunello di Montalcino, and is currently being planted in small quantities in a number of sites in California.

Syrah (Shiraz) For at least 200 years this has supplied superlative, full-bodied wines like Hermitage and Côte-Rôtie from the northern Rhône Valley but little comment was made about the variety. In the nineteenth century cuttings were taken from the Rhône to Australia where the grape had a variable career until the legendary Max Schubert, head winemaker at Penfold's, used it for the remarkable Grange Hermitage – now simply called Grange – which the acclaimed wine writer, Hugh Johnson, has named 'the greatest red in the southern hemisphere'. South African examples are beginning to win plaudits, with La Motte, Fleur du Cap and Fairview prominent.

Tannat A greatly under-rated variety, at its best in Madiran where there are a number of fine estates like Domaine Aydie. It is also found quite widely in the Jurançon and Irouléguy appellations in south-west France.

Tempranillo Best known as the most successful grape in the Rioja region of Spain, it is also a source of some attractive wines from the Costers del Segre area. In the Penedès it is blended by Miguel Torres in their Coronas wines. It is also popular in Argentina.

Zinfandel Best known in California where it has had a varied career. In the 1970s and 1980s it produced some over-heavy wines with excessively high alcoholic levels. More recently, many winemakers have taken considerable care to ensure better balanced wines. The Amador Valley is arguably the best source. Zinfandel is grown in some other New World countries but without widespread enthusiasm.

Simply Champagne

Le Champagne: the wine
La Champagne: the region

the region Champagne is the most northerly wine-producing region in France and lies on chalky soil similar to that found in the white cliffs of Dover. The Champagne trade is centred around the cities of Épernay and Reims and two hundred or so villages, some with delightful names like Dizy and Bouzy. There are three main vineyard areas – the Mountain of Reims, the Valley of the Marne and the Côte des Blancs – and two smaller areas to the south called Bar-sur-Aube and Bar-sur-Seine.

Most Champagne is aged for up to three years (some for much longer), in chalk caves about 30 metres (100 feet) underground. The bubbles come from a secondary fermentation deliberately started inside the bottles.

the largest Champagne house Moët et Chandon with around 21 million bottles a year.

the smallest Champagne producer This is difficult to quantify and is judged on the basis that the title should go to a *proprietaire-récoltant* whose sole living is obtained from selling Champagne produced entirely from his or her own vines. In these circumstances the smallest may be Nicole Martin of Champillon, who makes a maximum of 12,000 bottles a year in an extended garage under her bungalow.

the oldest Champagne house The house of Ruinart is generally acknowledged as the oldest. It was founded on 1 September 1729.

remuage or riddling The gradual turning and inverting of bottles shakes the sediment into their necks which are then frozen. The bottles are raised upright, the crown corks are removed and the pressure of the sparkling wine ejects an ice pellet of wine that contains the deposit. (See 'Colourful Characters': **Clicquot, Nicole Barbe**.)

dosage Immediately after the removal of the frozen sediment, during what is called the *liqueur d'expedition*, a small volume of cane sugar dissolved in old still wine is added to restore the level in the bottles. The amount of sugar in this 'dosage' controls the dryness of the final Champagne.

the swizzle stick The Romans developed glass rods for mixing drinks and the fashion reappeared in the United States. During the nineteenth century it became fashionable both there and in Britain to use coloured glass swizzle sticks to remove the bubbles from Champagne. Some people even stirred the wine in open jugs to achieve

the effect quickly. The result, of course, was a swizzle as the finest sparkling wines turned flat and lifeless.

LETTERS ON LABELS

CM = Cooperative-Manipulant Champagne made and marketed by a co-operative.

MA = Marque Auxiliare These letters indicate a second or subsidiary label of a Champagne house.

NM = Négociant-Manipulant Found on most exported Champagne bottles these letters identify what are generally known as Champagne houses. A *négoçiant-manipulant* is a producer who purchases either grapes or wine from other growers or producers and then uses them for all or part of his needs.

RM = Récoltant-Manipulant A grower who makes and markets his or her own wine. (See 'Winespeak': **Proprietaire-Récoltant**.)

LEVELS OF DRYNESS

brut zero/brut sauvage/brut non-dosage/ultra brut The driest of all styles with cane sugar levels of 0–6 g/l (0–6 grams per litre).

brut This means very dry (less than 15 g/l) and is the most popular style. It is also the level of dryness or sweetness which most experts acknowledge to be the finest for Champagne.

extra dry A slightly less dry style than Brut (12–20 g/l) which some houses, notably Pol Roger and G.H. Mumm, have perfected.

sec or dry This is little seen nowadays and traditionally has 17–35 g/l.

demi-sec/medium-dry Consumers should be warned that Champagne houses use their lesser *cuvées* or blends for sweeter Champagnes. If 33–50 g/l are added the true characteristics of the wine will not be appreciated.

doux/rich/sweet With more than 50 g/l this is the sweetest of all styles and will bring delight to those with the most sugary palates. The late Earl Spencer, who had particularly sweet taste buds, used to buy half-bottles of sweet Champagne from Louis Roederer and Pol Roger and age them for seven years. The result was golden, rich, unctuous bubbly but a long way from the finest quality.

THE CHAMPAGNE STYLES

Blanc de Blancs 100 per cent white Champagne from Chardonnay grapes. This style is delicious as an aperitif; Pol Roger is a consistently fine example.

rosé Champagne Occasionally – to the annoyance of some houses – called 'pink'. It is always vinified in a dry style and is available both in non-vintage and vintage Champagne. It is best drunk younger than white Champagne while it retains its fruit. Some is made by leaving the red skins of Pinot Noir and Pinot Meunier grapes in contact with the juice for a brief period. Other examples are vinified by blending the local red wine, Bouzy Rouge, or other red Coteaux

Champenois with white Champagne. Both styles have their followers.

non-vintage Around 80 per cent of the Champagne sold by the larger houses is non-vintage. Basically a non-vintage *cuvée* comprises wine from one harvest to which a small volume of reserve wine, which may come from one or more older years, has been added.

vintage Champagne This long-ageing style has steadily diminished in popularity in the last two decades. In the past it was made only from those vintages which were judged the finest and often vinified to appreciate slow cellar-ageing. The development of prestige labels has seen buyers preferring to choose these or non-vintage blends.

prestige or luxury cuveés The terms prestige and luxury are used differently by different houses and writers. These are specially selected wines, usually made exclusively from grapes grown in the finest vineyards in the most highly-rated villages. In most instances they are not released until they are five or more years of age.

SOME OUTSTANDING PRESTIGE LABELS

Comtes de Champagne 100 per cent Blanc de Blancs, it is the prestige label of Champagne Taittinger and a well-favoured style.

Dom Pérignon The prestige style of the giant Moët et Chandon house which has been especially fine in recent vintages despite its large volume. It was first launched in 1933 when Prohibition ended in the United States.

La Grande Dame The very title refers to the Widow Clicquot and it is, of course, the extremely agreeable luxury style of Champagne Veuve Clicquot.

Louis Roederer Cristal The oldest luxury *cuvée*, originally the exclusive Champagne of Alexander II of Russia (see 'Stories'). The white is a magnificent Champagne that is remarkably consistent, while some cognoscenti prefer the house's standard rosé blend to its Cristal Rosé.

Perrier-Jouët Belle Epoque or Fleur de Champagne Introduced in 1968, this is better known to many *aficionados* as 'the flower bottle'. It is claimed, with some justification, that it represents the finest art both outside and inside the bottle. Each anemone-covered bottle is hand-crafted and baked in a small oven at 500°C. The 1985 'flower bottle' won the Grappe d'Or award of *Gault-Millau* magazine for the outstanding wine of that vintage.

Salon le Mesnil This unique Champagne is only ever made from 100 per cent Chardonnay grapes and during the finest vintages. It is aged on its lees for a minimum of nine years and the youngest Salon released often has 12 or more years of age. It is the ultimate luxury in Champagne terms and every lover of the wine should permit him/herself to indulge in it at least once in a lifetime. If the angels do drink Champagne in heaven, surely it must be Salon? (See also pages 57–8, **the case of the cellar master's murder**.)

Sir Winston Churchill This luxury style of Champagne Pol Roger was launched with the 1979 vintage and reflects the house's close relationship with the great man and his family, and his enjoyment of long-ageing Champagne.

Blanc des Millenaires 'White of the millennium'. The award-winning prestige style of Champagne Charles Heidsieck which matures superbly.

Le Grand Siècle The full-flavoured prestige *cuvée* of Champagne Laurent Perrier has probably received less praise than it deserves. The rosé version can be most attractive.

Winespeak

A

Abboccato Italian term for medium-dry wine.

Alcohol Alcohol in wine is a result of the fermentation of grape juice and can be measured in various ways. Yeast enzymes convert grape sugar into alcohol and give off carbon dioxide. The word is Arab in origin and refers to the distillation process used to produce kohl.

American oak Chiefly from Missouri where wild trees are cut and the timber seasoned. It has a rougher, more pitted surface than most European oak which comes from smaller trees in forests that have often been cultivated for centuries. Wines with longer ageing potential normally develop their flavours at a quicker rate when matured in American oak, which is also renowned for its vanilla bouquet.

Amontillado A style of Sherry, whose name is derived from its similarity to some fortified wines from Montilla. Two different qualities appear to have developed in recent years: mass-produced Finos which have been brought to a popular medium-sweet level by the addition of Pedro Ximinez grapes; and increasingly rare 'true' amontillados, which are never available in any quantity and which require seven to eight years ageing and strengthening with older wines.

Appellation Contrôlée (AC) The French control system which regulates grape varieties, minimum and maximum alcoholic strength, yield per hectare and basic winemaking style(s) for named geographical regions. For example, the wine of Muscadet de Sèvre-et-Maine can only be vinified from Melon de Bourgogne grapes to a minimum of 9° and a maximum of 12° (alcohol by volume). The maximum production permitted is 40 hectolitres (4000 litres) per hectare and the style must be still white.

Ausbruch An ancient style of sweet wine first made at Rust in Burgenland, Austria, a region that was part of Hungary before 1921. It comes between Beerenauslese and Trockenbeerenauslese in sweetness and is produced by adding fresh grape must to some that has already been crushed from grapes affected by noble rot.

Auslese Term used in Austria and Germany for outstanding sweet wines. They are pressed from individually late-picked bunches of extremely ripe grapes that exceed the required Oechsle level (See 'Winespeak O').

barco rabelo An unusual, small wooden river craft used for centuries on the Douro river in Portugal to ferry Port from the vineyards upstream to the ageing lodges of Vila Nova da Gaia. A high platform allowed the tillerman to avoid dangerous rapids. An annual race is still held between the Port houses but otherwise the boats are retained only for publicity and tourism.

baumé A French scale for measuring musts and sweet white wines.

Beerenauslese German word for wine pressed from individually selected, late-picked bunches of white grapes. A higher oechsle level is required than for auslese.

bin An English word, originally used for the section of a cellar where a particular wine or vintage was stored. It is often used nowadays to indicate a particular vat or blend of wine.

Blanc de Noirs Sparkling (and very occasionally still) wines made using only black grapes. The term refers to their white flesh.

blend A much misunderstood term which indicates that various wines have been mixed to make one better-balanced wine. Major houses often do this to provide consistency from year to year. In Champagne almost all non-vintage bottles contain blends produced from the wines of many different villages.

brix A scale of measurement for the level of natural sugar in grapes, widely used in the New World.

$$\mathcal{C}$$

caves The name widely used for underground cellars in France.

chais The name generally given to cellars built above the ground in France.

château A vineyard or wine estate upon which there should be a habitable building that can provide identification. Many châteaux are tiny and virtually unknown, others are substantial, magnificent and famous. The Bordeaux region alone has some 4000 wine châteaux.

Claret Term for red Bordeaux. Derived from old French *Clairet*, a pinkish wine which was produced many centuries ago when skins were not kept in contact with their juice long enough to provide adequate colour.

clos In France traditionally an individual vineyard enclosed by walls.

crianza A Spanish term that means nursery wine. Often seen on Rioja and other labels, it normally signifies that a red wine has been aged for a minimum of 12 months in oak and is ready for immediate drinking.

cuvée French for blend. In Champagne, once the still wines have completed their first fermentation the tasters blend as many as a hundred or more still wines to make up the *cuvée*. This blend of still wines is put into separate bottles for the secondary fermentation to take place.

Decanter Classic wine magazine founded in London by Colin Parnell and Tony Lord in 1975. The opinions of its contributors and tasting panels are greatly respected.

demi-sec Essentially the French term for medium-dry but experts argue about the difference between medium-dry and medium-sweet. The latter is hardly ever seen. Demi-sec on a Champagne label definitely implies medium-sweet.

deposit Another word for natural sediment, more often found in red than white wines. In whites it is normally composed of tartaric acid crystals and is tasteless and harmless, but it can be tannic and bitter in reds. Bottles with deposits should be placed upright for a week before they are drunk and then decanted or poured carefully. It is important to watch the deposit to ensure it does not move into the main flow.

domaine Word used in much of France for an estate. The exceptions are Bordeaux and many parts of the Loire or south-west, where château, the simple identification *propriétaire*, or even *mas* are preferred.

doux French for sweet.

dry Generally used to describe wines with the lowest natural sugar content.

ℰ

Eiswein (or ice wine) Late-picked, sweet white wine, made in Germany, Austria and Canada, usually in November or December from grapes that are frozen solid when they are harvested. In Germany regulations require temperatures at the time of picking to be between –8°C (14°F) and –10°C (18°F). The procedure often involves small groups of dedicated pickers gathering carefully selected bunches before sunrise. The freezing causes the water content, in the form of ice, to separate from the grape juice leaving the latter dense and rich.

English and Welsh wines The naming of this category was altered when the 1995 English Wine of the Year title was awarded to Cariad from Pendoylan in Wales. Some 400 hectares (988 acres) of vineyards are spread across the southern part of Great Britain, most of them relatively small properties. Denbies Vineyard at Dorking Surrey, is the largest at 107 hectares (264 acres) while many are less than one hectare (2½ acres). The inconsistent climate is the greatest problem and most wine producers persist in growing safety-first hybrids rather than noble varieties. However, a few small experiments with the latter are beginning to produce encouraging results.

estate The use of this word on labels has become confused. Some experts say it should signify that a wine has been made only from grapes grown on the property whose name is on the label. This tradition is still observed in South Africa, but in Australia some estates buy grapes from various states and make several wines that are blended to make a south-eastern Australian wine. The owners argue, often with some justification, that by selecting the finest grapes available from a number of growers they are producing better wine than would be possible if they used only their own.

esters Components of wine which influence its bouquet and aroma.

Factory House An historic eighteenth-century building in Oporto, Portugal, which is home to the British Association, an exclusive all-male organisation restricted to the partners of the 12 British-owned Port houses. The highlight of its Wednesday lunch, one of the few occasions when guests are permitted, is the blind tasting of a vintage Port when many of the world's greatest experts demonstrate their fallibility.

fattoria Italian word for a farm or estate.

fermentation The conversion of grape juice into wine. This occurs when yeast reacts with grape sugar to form ethyl alcohol and carbon dioxide.

filtration The clarification of wine. This is normally carried out immediately before bottling, usually through *kieselguhr* or *millipore* filters which are so efficient that they can remove particles invisible to the human eye.

fining The clarification of wine just after its fermentation. A wide variety of materials is used ranging from fresh egg whites to bentonite, gelatine and dried blood.

finish The last flavour that remains on the palate after drinking a wine. The finish of the greatest wines can often be appreciated hours after consuming them.

Fino The driest and often the finest style of Sherry and Montilla. It should always be served chilled, ideally with *tapas*.

flor A natural white yeast that forms on the surface of Fino and Manzanilla Sherries as they age in butts. When Alexander Fleming was carrying out his research into penicillin he visited the Domecq bodegas in Jerez to examine the *flor*. Vested interests once assured wine lovers that it occurred naturally only in three wine regions of Europe. However, it also exists in parts of South Africa and California and no doubt elsewhere.

flying winemaker A winemaker who flies between various countries supervising wine production, especially at vintage time. Many introduce New World techniques to regions with traditional practices. The best-known names include Peter Bright and John Worontscheck from Australia, Kym Milne from New Zealand and Hugh Ryman, from France but of English heritage.

fortified wine A term that covers white and red wines to which neutral alcohol or young grape brandy has been added for two reasons: to enhance the style; and to raise the alcohol level. Port, Sherry, Madeira, Malaga, Montilla, Marsala and various Muscats are the most widely seen examples.

foxy A word, considered derogatory by many Europeans, used to describe a strange flavour common among wines made from the native American *labrusca* species of vine.

French oak Widely used for ageing fine wine. Its narrow pores mean the wine matures slowly and will continue to do so in bottle. Allier, Limousin, Nevers and Tronçais are the main forests.

frizzante Italian for lightly sparkling.

galets Large, flat, oval-shaped pebbles found in the Vaucluse region of France which was once covered by a prehistoric sea. The most notable examples are found in Châteauneuf-du-Pape. The pebbles absorb the heat of the sun during the day and radiate it at night, thus encouraging the vines to grow.

garrafeira Portuguese word indicating that the wine has had long bottle-ageing.

giro-pallette An automatic *remuage* or riddling machine which shakes cases of sparkling wine during a pre-selected series of times and durations.

goût de terroir French expression indicating an earthy taste; to the extent that which a wine's flavour is influenced by the soil in which the vines have grown.

grafting Most American rootstocks are resistant to phylloxera and by grafting other cuttings on to them the entire plant becomes resistant while taking on the variety of the cutting.

Grand Cru French term that refers to the official rating of an outstanding vineyard. Its importance varies. For instance in Alsace many consider that there are an excessive number of Grand Crus and decline to use the term. In Bordeaux the longer term Grand Cru Classé is usually an essential guide.

Grand Cru Classé A Bordeaux term classifying wines. They were rated in 1855 by a committee who calculated the wholesale prices of the leading wines over the previous 30 years and then listed them accordingly. It has been standard practice since 1855 for UK writers to translate the French Grand Cru Classé as First Growth, Second Growth etc, depending on the actual rating. There are five growths in all.

halbtrocken 'Medium-dry'. A German wine style that has grown increasingly popular domestically but made little impression in export markets.

hard A term that means a wine is uncompromising and lacking subtlety or softness. This can sometimes be overcome with ageing.

haut French word for 'higher,' 'upper' or 'more northerly'. For example, in Château Haut-Smith-Lafitte *lafitte* means the best area, Smith is the founder's name and *haut* implies the highest part of the land.

hectare Ancient measure for an area of 10,000 square metres, the equivalent of 2.47 acres.

Hock An English term, now less widely used than previously, which generally covers all Rhine wines. It derives from Queen Victoria's predilection for wines from the village of Hochheim.

𝒥

ice wine See Eiswein ('Winespeak E').

irrigation A matter for debate by fine-wine traditionalists but perfectly acceptable to most modern winemakers. Irrigation is widely practised in the New World where climatic conditions often make it essential. It is often achieved by a system of narrow pipes that run along the rows of vines. The main purpose is to ensure that the plants receive the optimum volume of water – not the maximum, which would make the wine too thin.

isinglass A fining agent used for both wines and beers. It is extracted from the bladders of certain sturgeons.

J

Jerez The Spanish town Jerez de la Frontera from which we get the word Sherry. It was once a frontier between the Christian and Muslim worlds.

K

Kabinett Sometimes seen as Cabinet on older vintages. It is the first level of German *prädikat* wine or Qmp and has enough natural sugar to make it unnecessary to add any *süssreserve* or sweet grape juice to bolster the quality.

kimmeridge A unique layer of clay and limestone soil that begins in Kimmeridge, Dorset, then dips below the English Channel before reappearing in the premier and Grand Cru vineyards of Chablis.

kosher wine Wine made according to rabbinical hygiene laws. It usually involves rabbis and other approved Orthodox Jews attending the vintage on a particular day to ensure that all the regulations are observed. It does not usually taste any different from other wines from the same source.

Labrusca The most widely seen of the native North American vine species, it is responsible for 'foxy' wines. (see **Foxy**).

landwein The German equivalent of the French *vin de pays* or country wine.

larmes, les French for tears, a term for the glycerine that clings to a glass and shows that a wine has the potential to age.

latte French word for a strip of wood that is laid between individual rows of bottles left to age in a cellar.

lees Another term for sediment. Some winemakers give much credence to ageing their wine on the lees as this is said to give it freshness and vitality. Muscadet Sur Lie is an example.

length Indicates how long the taste of a wine lingers on the palate.

light A term of approval with some elegant white wines. However, it is generally derogatory with reds when it suggests a lack of colour, alcohol and body.

liquoreux French word meaning sweet and rich, used to describe white wines.

liquoroso Italian description for a fortified dessert wine.

lodge The English form of the Portuguese *loja*, an above-ground cellar.

maceration The process whereby the fermenting grape juice or must remains in contact with the skins. With white wines this may not take place at all, with rosé wines it may last anything from nine to 36 hours and with reds it is usually several days or even longer. In general terms the longer the time, the deeper the colour of the end product.

maderised A term indicating that a wine has oxidised and decayed, giving a foul, slightly burnt taste. It should never be consumed as it will make you feel most uncomfortable.

Maître de chais French for cellar master.

méthode-traditionelle A term for sparkling wines vinified by bottle fermentation in the way traditionally associated with Champagne, introduced and enforced by the European Union. Krone Borealis and Boschendal from South Africa, Seppelt Salinger, Seaview Pinot Noir-Chardonnay and Croser from Australia, Roederer Estate from California, Argyll from Oregon and Gratien Cuvée Flamme from Saumur, France, are among the most attractive bottles widely available.

millésime French for vintage year.

mis en bouteilles au château (or domaine) Château or estate-bottled.

moelleux French description of a particular taste, translated in a number of ways. Many producers say that the term means a wine has the sweetness and texture of marrow – some tasters argue for bone marrow and others for the vegetable variety. Moelleux does not necessarily mean that a wine will be sweet. The characteristic is most commonly found in the finest vintages of white Loire wines such as Vouvray, Bonnezeaux, Quarts de Chaume and Coteaux du Layon.

mousse The bubbling action of sparkling wines.

mousseux French for 'sparkling'; not used in Champagne.

must The juice of grapes that have just been crushed.

mutage French word for the addition of alcohol or sulphur dioxide to wine to stop fermentation, often to make a *vin doux naturel*, or fortified sweet wine.

N

négociant A merchant who buys and sells wines in the wholesale markets and bottles some or many of them. In Bordeaux a *négociant* may buy bulk Bordeaux AC from one producer and sell it to another *négociant* who may blend it with other, similar, wines to supply the needs of a major brand. *Négociants* usually also hold large stocks of the wines of their regions which they have blended and bottled. A *négociant-eleveur* ages wines before selling them. Most *négociants* today cover both roles, at least to some degree.

nitrogen Widely used to protect wine from oxidisation. In many cellars the wine in part-filled vats is covered with a blanket of the gas. Some bars and restaurants that serve fine wines by the glass have machines that use nitrogen.

Noble Rot/Botrytis Cinerea/Pourriture Noble/Edelfaule The celebrated fungus which penetrates the skins of white grapes for sweet wines and consumes the water content of the juice causing it to become concentrated. As late as 1985 wine writers were saying that the most successful regions for noble rot were Sauternes and Bonnezeaux in France, parts of the Mosel and Rheingau in Germany and Tokaji in Hungary. Since then Burgenland in Austria has restored an ancient tradition and produces some fine noble-rot wines, and similar wines of consistent quality have been made in several New World countries.

non-vintage A wine that is not identified as coming from any particular vintage. The use of the term is decreasing.

nose To smell a wine; or the term can be used to identify the bouquet and aroma.

nouveau Most familiar when linked with Beaujolais, it indicates the first wine of a new vintage. Nouveau wines are party wines and should never be taken too seriously. *Primeur* has the same meaning.

oechsle German measurement of the specific gravity of grape juice which indicates the potential alcohol; the higher the reading the better. When, in Germany, growers deliver their grapes to brokers, co-operatives or merchants for crushing, their juice is measured in *oechsle* and they are paid accordingly.

oeil de perdrix The phrase translates literally as 'the eye of the partridge' which, of course, is bloodshot. It used to denote a style, mostly found in Champagne, when red grape skins gave a pinkish hue to the wine.

oenology (pronounced 'eenology') Wine science. Oenologists play vital roles in wine production and in recent years have been responsible for overall consistency, reliable standards and substantial improvements in quality in some countries.

oloroso Generally the richest and fullest of Sherry styles, it usually has a nutty taste. When blended with Pedro Ximénez grapes it produces some of the more popular Cream Sherries.

organic wines Unfortunately there are no widely recognised international standards for these. In principle organic means that chemicals are not used in the vineyard and sulphur dioxide is forbidden in the wine cellar, but few who claim to produce organic wines can confirm total abstention from these practices. All the world's greatest wines use sulphur dioxide and no organic wine has yet been able to claim greatness. On the contrary, many are disappointing. Exceptions are those produced by Fetzer Vineyards at Valley Oaks in California and Penfold's Chardonnay-Sauvignon Blanc from the Clare Valley in South Australia.

oxidised See **maderised**.

petit château A wine-trade term for the 4000 or so little-known chateaux in the Bordeaux region that vinify their wines in an early maturing style. They can be excellent purchases in great vintages and are generally agreeable in most years.

phylloxera See 'Great Wine Disasters'

plonk From the Cockney rhyming slang 'plink plonk, vin blanc', perhaps developed by Londoners who served as soldiers in the First World War.

pressing The process of extracting the juice from the grapes by pressing or crushing them. This can be achieved in various ways, including treading, but pneumatic presses are probably the most popular method today. The grapes are pressed by a giant inflatable bag, rather like an inner tube, within a metal container. This prevents harsh bruising and diminishes the risk of oxidation.

proprietaire-recoltant French for a small grower who also produces his or her own wine.

pruning An annual necessity to remove excessive wood from vines and encourage strong growth for the next year. It usually starts about two months after the picking and lasts until about two months before the new flowering is due.

puttonyos A measured Hungarian bucket used to add hand-picked, over-ripe grapes to the press-ing during the production of Tokaji Aszu. The more *puttonyos* printed on the label, the more concentrated the wine. The levels are normally between two and six.

QbA or Qualitatswein bestimmer Anbaugeit The next level above basic *tafelwein* or table wine in Germany. It is made in 11 official regions from specified grape varieties and *süssreserve* may be added to it. Those seeking better quality German wines are advised to start with the Kabinett level of Qmp wines.

quinta Portuguese for a farm or country property. The marketing of vintage Ports from single *quintas* is a growing fashion.

QmP or Qualitatswein mit Pradikat Wines from grapes that have ripened sufficiently and have enough grape sugar to make the addition of *süssreserve* unnecessary. There are five categories, controlled by *oechsle* (potential sweetness) levels: Kabinett, Spätlese, Auslese, Beerenauslese and Trockenbeerenauslese (see individual listings in 'Winespeak'). These terms are used in both Austria and Germany.

racking The transfer of wine from a barrel where it has been maturing to another cask. This takes place several times during vinification.

rancio An oxidised style of fortified wine.

reserva A Spanish term for a red wine that has been aged in oak for a minimum of 12 months and cannot be shipped or sold until its fourth year. Many good producers add extra time. The

wines are made only from the better years and the vintage should always be on the label.

reserva (Portugal)
Compared with Spain fewer controls apply. In effect, the term implies a superior, well-aged red wine with a minimum alcohol level at least 0.5 per cent above the norm. It is best to rely on a reputable producer.

residual sugar
The natural grape sugar that remains in a wine once fermentation has been exhausted.

riserva Italian term for a red wine that has been aged for longer than normal. Regulations vary depending upon the individual DOC (Denominazione di Origine Controllata, the Italian equivalent of the French AC). The title Riserva Speciale is given to wines with even longer ageing but again there are local sets of regulations to be observed.

Sack Theories that 'Sack' is derived from the Spanish *seco* for dry seem to be inaccurate. The earliest written records come from the fifteenth and sixteenth centuries and refer to Malaga Sack, Canary Sack and Sherry Sack, all of which were sweet wines. The word comes from the Spanish *sacar*, to go out or ship, and refers to wine exported from those regions. Sack was a favourite tipple of Shakespeare's Sir John Falstaff. Dry Sack from Williams & Humbert is an extremely popular label but, unlike its early predecessors, is medium-dry.

sacramental wine The need for wine for Holy Communion was largely responsible for vineyards spreading through Europe and their establishment in various parts of the New World. In South Africa many early settlers insisted that as it represented the 'blood of Christ' only red wine should be used. In the British Isles and much of North America specially commissioned, fortified wine has often been used, while in Cyprus it has always been the practice to use local wines given to the church as offerings. In California the first sacramental wines were crushed by hired Indians who trod them in large barrels.

schloss The German word for château, its use is decreasing.

sec/secco French and Italian for dry.

second wine A practice, which is increasing, whereby châteaux and estates reserve their best grapes for their finest wines and use lesser, but perfectly acceptable, crops for second labels. For example, Château Margaux markets Pavillon de Margaux, and Château Cantemerle makes Baron Villeneuve de Cantemerle. These can make out-standing purchases in the greatest vintages and are otherwise consistently good.

sediment See **deposit**.

sekt A German word for sparkling wine.

short A critical term which indicates that a wine has no real finish and is lacking in most necessary characteristics.

soft Originally used to describe a gentle wine that displays no firmness when it is first made and is unlikely to age well. Nowadays it is used to describe a wine with a little residual sugar which makes it easy on the palate.

soil In general terms poor soils encourage good wines and rich soils are likely to produce dull and indifferent results. The type of soil in a vineyard is one of the main factors that determines a wine's characteristics. The chalky limestone of Champagne and the *terra rossa* of Australia's Coonawarra region are contrasting examples.

solera The standard system of barrel-ageing used for Sherry, Malaga and some Madeira. A *solera* comprises four rows of butts, one row resting on another, in descending order of age: the youngest wines are on the top and the most mature on the ground.

   The wines are poured from one row to the next, gradually blending with each other as they age. Although some *soleras* claim to have been started in the nineteenth century this does not mean that the wine is any better than later blends as any trace of the early vintage must have long since departed.

sommelier French term for a wine waiter or wine steward. The master sommelier qualification has become highly respected around the world.

sparkling wine Although Champagne is a sparkling wine it is not usually listed under that category. The term covers all other wines that contain bubbles obtained by one of several methods. These are the *méthode-traditionelle*, formerly known as the *méthode-champenoise*, the transfer method, the Charmat or cuve close method and the carbonation method. The *méthode-traditionelle* involves secondary fermentation in the bottles, as in Champagne. The transfer method also includes this but the wine is then transferred to large vats for the sediment to be removed, rather than going through the *remuage* process. The Charmat method has secondary fermentation in a sealed vat and the carbonation method means the addition of piped gas.

Spätlese Late picked. In Germany and parts of Austria the term implies that the grapes have ripened better than those picked earlier because of longer exposure to the sun. Spätlese is one stage sweeter than Kabinett and could generally be called medium-sweet.

spritzig A German term meaning 'lightly sparkling'. It is widely used to describe the sensation when a taster is able to detect minor bubbles that tingle on the end of the tongue.

spumante Italian for sparkling.

stalky A term for certain big red wines that have excess tannin from the grape stalks.

sulphur and sulphur dioxide Two of the most misunderstood agents in wine production. In some countries sulphur is widely used in vineyards to protect vines against oidium – a type of fungus – and before wooden casks are used sulphur tablets are burnt inside them. Sulphuring is a hygienic practice that eradicates wild yeasts and unwanted bacteria that cause wine to deteriorate. It also prevents fermenting grape must oxidising. Its final use is in bottles to fill the space between the wine and the cork and so prevent oxidisation. A number of attempts are under way to produce and market organic wines without the use of sulphur but few producers can claim total abstention. A tiny fraction of wine drinkers may occasionally have an adverse reaction to sulphur.

sundial The construction of vineyard sundials was once a practice in various regions. The best-known examples are in Germany's Mosel Valley where only three remain, the most famous of which is the Wehlener Sonnenhur. The position of the sundials is always a good guide to the ripest grapes and subsequently the finest wine, for they always stood where the sun gave the best exposure at noon, the time when vineyard workers took their lunch break.

supérieur French term indicating wine with a higher minimum alcohol level than the basic Appellation Contrôlée of a particular region. For example, Bordeaux AC requires a minimum of 10.0° while Bordeaux Supérieur must be at least 10.5°. The term often indicates a better wine.

superiore Italian term of similar application to *supérieur*.

sur lie See lees ('Winespeak L').

süssreserve 'Sweet reserve'. Usually unfermented grape juice from the previous vintage. In northern Europe it is added to wines that are below the permitted minimum strength levels to enable them to reach the required standards. Disciplined use helps to produce large volumes of quaffable, everyday wines. Some question whether it should be permitted for the Auslese level where the name implies natural sweetness.

sweet wine The finest sweet wines are pressed only from late-picked, over-ripe grapes. In the best vintages many will have noble rot. Lesser sweet wines are made by adding sugar or by stopping the fermentation before all the grape sugar has been converted to alcohol.

table wine A term that has become somewhat confused but which basically means wines for everyday consumption rather than fine ones. It is seldom used to describe sparkling wines.

tafelwein The most basic category of German wine.

tannin An essential component of red wines, which usually means that they will age well.

Tannin is an extract from the skins, pips and stalks of grapes and when found in abundance in a young wine, one which still needs to develop, tends to stick to the back of the teeth.

tartar See **deposit**.

tawny A style of Port with a tawny colour, the result of being aged in wood for anything from four to 30 or more years. The finest tawnies always state their age on their labels. Once shipped, Tawny Port is not intended for cellaring but for early consumption. It can be delightful well chilled.

tears (or legs) See **Larmes, les**.

tinto Spanish for red.

tough A term which describes a wine that possesses too much tannin but which is likely to balance well with maturity.

trocken Introduced in the early 1980s to recognise a new style of German dry wine. It has not had much success in the export market as it is often too low in alcohol and too frail in structure.

Trockenbeerenauslese Sweet wine made from late-picked, individually selected grapes that must have noble rot. Found in Austria and Germany, it is rather expensive as it is labour intensive and may be produced only every ten or so years when outstanding climatic conditions have continued into late autumn. It ages exceedingly well. Its taste can be quite memorable and can remain on the palate hours later.

U

ullage The space between the cork and the surface of a wine. When an auctioneer says a wine has been 'ullaged', he is drawing attention to the fact that the level of wine in the bottle has dropped. Ullaging should happen only very slowly and be consistent with great age. A young wine that is ullaged should be avoided as this generally suggests cork problems.

V

varietal A wine identified by the name of a grape variety on its label. Its use is not always consistent. In California the naming of a variety on a label means that it represents a minimum of 75 per cent of the wine while in France it must be 100 per cent. In fairness to California the addition of a minor proportion of another variety can enhance a wine – but why not always say so?

vat The common term for any large storage tank or barrel. It can be made of various woods, stainless steel, fibre glass or even concrete.

VDQS Vin Délimité de Qualité Supérieur, the official category below Appellation Contrôlée in France. With the rise in quality and popularity of *vin de pays* it is losing its significance.

vecchio An Italian term for old which implies that the wine has been aged in cellars.

vendange The harvesting or picking of the grapes in France.

vendange tardive Alsace term for white wines pressed from late-picked grapes. They can be dry, medium or sweet and can be sold only after 1½ years ageing. The best houses normally keep them a little longer.

vendemmia Italian for *vendange*.

Vermouth A wine-based aperitif flavoured with herbs, spices and wood barks. One particular bark, *vermud* or wormwood, which was widely used in past centuries, gave the drink its name. The ancient kingdom of Savoy (which included today's Savoie region of France and had its capital in Turin), has for centuries been the centre of Vermouth production.

vigneron French term for a wine producer.

vin doux naturel French term for a naturally sweet wine whose fermentation has been halted by *mutage* – the addition of neutral grape alcohol which also fortifies it. Leading examples are Muscat de Beaumes de Venise, Muscat de Frontignan, Banyuls, Rivesaltes and Maury.

vin de pays Introduced in 1981, this French category of country wines has proved a considerable success. The giant vin de pays d'Oc in the south of France has seen massive grubbing out of uninspiring vines and large-scale planting of noble varieties like Chardonnay and Merlot.

Vinho Verde The so called 'green wine' of Portugal, most of which comes from the north. It is made from slightly under-ripe grapes which leave a little more acidity than usual. The wines are usually slightly *petillant* and can be very refreshing in a warm climate, if well chilled. Many come in traditional, oval glass flasks.

vinification The production of wine from pressing to ageing.

Vin Santo An Italian dessert wine, often at its finest in Tuscany. Traditionally made Vin Santo is aged in small casks, *caratellie*, which are placed in the roof spaces of farms and large houses where their maturing is accelerated by constant changes of temperature. Sadly, some larger firms market certain examples which have not benefited from this ageing, something which is obvious from the dullness of the wines. Vin Santo can be dry or sweet.

vintage A widely used term which means the harvest and also the year of the harvest. In the northern hemisphere the earliest harvests normally begin in the second week of July at Fort Stockton in Texas and in rare cases some late-picked German wines have been harvested in January of the following year. In the southern hemisphere, the Twee Jonge Gezellen estate at Tulbagh in South Africa's Western Cape has reported the possibility of starting the January harvest in the last few days of December but has not put this into effect as doing so would cause dating complications. Very little southern wine is picked after April.

vintage character A commercial term for the better, more mature ruby Ports that have been aged for four or five years and offer something of the character of vintage Port.

Vintage Port The finest style of Port, it is produced only in the best years which are later declared as vintages by the individual Port houses. Houses sometimes disagree and select different years. Vintage Port is a fortified red wine that is bottled after two years without filtration and continues to age for many years. Great names include Taylor, Graham, Dow, Warre, Offley Boa Vista, Quinta do Noval and Cockburns.

vintitulist The strange word for a collector of wine labels. What was once an intriguing hobby has become an enormous undertaking because of the hundreds of thousands of labels on the international markets.

viticulteur French word for vine-grower. If it is printed on a label it means that the grower has produced his own wine.

viticulture The cultivation of vines to provide grapes for the production of wine. The term covers all practices between breaking ground in a new vineyard to picking the grapes.

VQPRD A European Union term that has been widely recognised in Italy but not elsewhere. It stands for Vin de Qualité Produit dans une Région Déterminée – a quality wine produced in a specific region.

W

weingut Not the equivalent of a beer gut but a descriptive word for a wine estate or property in Germany.

White Port Originally a fairly sweet style of Port pressed from white grapes. In recent years it has generally been somewhat drier.

wine The fermented juice of grapes.

wine lake Euro-slang for the now-diminishing surplus wine production within the European Union that is distilled to produce industrial alcohol.

wine museums Many house ancient and curious artefacts. Harvey's has an excellent wine museum at Denmark Street in Bristol, the Martini Wine Museum at Pessione in Italy contains remarkable wine vessels over 2000 years old and Château Mouton-Rothschild has a most impressive art collection.

winery Widely accepted modern word for the place where a wine is produced.

Y

yeast The natural bloom on grapes. However, this can also contain certain wild yeasts that are likely to spoil the winemaking process. Winemakers are increasingly using cultivated wine yeasts that they can control more easily.

yield The quantity of grapes grown in any one year from a measured plot of land. In France the Appellation Contrôlée regulations restrict its size. In the New World growers are free to have any yield they wish but have generally long since learned that excessive yields create lower quality wines and winemakers therefore impose their own disciplines.

zapatos Hobnailed leather boots traditionally worn for stamping grapes in Spain's Sherry region.

zymase The enzymes in wine yeasts that convert grape sugar into alcohol and carbon dioxide.

Helpful Advice for Beginners

THE 40% RULE

Diners whose knowledge of wine is limited may feel apprehensive when dealing with a wine waiter/steward or sommelier. Most wine waiters wish only to help but a small proportion can be conscious of sales incentives. So a simple recommendation, when confronted with a large list in a fashionable restaurant, is to decide in advance whether to order a white, for example, Chardonnay or a red such as Merlot.

If you choose Chardonnay:

1 Tell the wine waiter that you need help and are sure he, or she, has plenty of expertise.
2 Ask approximately how many Chardonnays, including any French wines that may not display the varietal's name, are on the list.
3 Ask the wine waiter to choose the best value Chardonnay in the lowest 40 per cent (pricewise) of the list.

The waiter will not wish to seem critical of the quality of any wines which the restaurant stocks and will usually go out of his or her way to choose one of outstanding value.

Don't be a stick-in-the-mud. Experiment, even if you haven't a clue.

Start by going into the nearest multiple wine retailer and asking for help. Explain that you are a beginner and would like the manager to select three bottles for you. You wish to try:

1 A lower-priced medium-dry white from a European country.
2 A mid-priced red from Australia.
3 A slightly higher-priced dry white from North or South America.

Next, buy yourself a Vacu-Vin wine saver pump. This will allow you to try a glass of each wine and keep the remainder fresh for a further tasting. Your investment will prove worthwhile within a few weeks as wines that would otherwise have oxidised will not be wasted.

The following day try a half-glass of each of the wines with food, which is how most wine is enjoyed. Do be sure that they are at the appropriate temperature. Right from the start make yourself the most important wine judge; only you know what suits your palate. Keep a small notebook and on each occasion jot down the wine's name and give it a mark out of ten based on your appreciation of it and bearing in mind its price. Value for money is the golden rule. Then a couple of days later, repeat the exercise, with entirely different food. Two days later repeat the exercise again.

The next week visit a different retailer and

introduce yourself in the same manner, but this time ask for:

1 A lower-priced red from Europe.
2 A mid-priced dry white from South Africa.
3 A slightly higher-priced sparkling wine from Australia.

Continue this practice for four weeks and include an attractive independent retailer if possible. Keep all your marks carefully. Read them thoroughly and you will soon find:

1 Where your personal taste buds lie.
2 Where you believe the finest value wines are found.
3 Which retailer stocks the best selection, for you, in the price ranges given above.

S U G A R S   O R   S W E E T E N E R S

The following guidelines will indicate some – but not all – wine styles that are likely to suit the taste buds of about 90 per cent of wine drinkers. A few individuals, of course, may well have truly catholic palates that give them the pleasure of appreciating all sweetness levels and styles.

1 If you have not taken either sugar or sweeteners in coffee or tea for some while you have a truly dry palate and in white wines will probably prefer Sauvignon Blanc (but not many Californian examples), Pouilly Fumé, Sancerre, Graves Blanc Sec, some finer Chardonnays, most Alsace wines, Verdelho or Chenin Blanc from Western Australia, Viognier, Pinot Blanc (Bianco), Muscadet Sur Lie, Torrontés from

Argentina and Brut Champagne or most
méthode-traditionelle sparkling wines. Tavel,
Lirac and Menetou-Salon offer classic dry rosés
and Côtes de Provence supplies rosés of a
similar dryness that are very quaffable in warm
weather. For reds, try Cabernet Sauvignon,
Cabernet Franc, most Bordeaux châteaux and
other classic French reds; also Rioja, Ribera del
Duero and Penedès from Spain; Dão Reservas,
Torres Vedras and most other Portuguese reds;

most traditional Italian reds; Naoussa from Greece and Château Musar from the Lebanon.

2   If you take one sugar or sweetener with coffee or tea you have a soft-dry palate and in white wines may well be more comfortable with inexpensive New World Chardonnay or dry Riesling from Australia, Chenin Blanc from the New World or Vouvray, its best-known French appellation, Californian Sauvignon Blanc which tends to have a little more residual sugar than most, Trocken wines from Germany or Pinot Grigio from Italy. Among sparkling wines, many Australian or Californian examples, or many Spanish *Cavas*, will suit. In reds, Merlot, Shiraz or Syrah, Pinot Noir, Dolcetto from Italy and Pamid and Mavrud from Bulgaria should please.

3   Consumers of two sugars or sweeteners have medium-sweet taste buds and will enjoy most German wines at the low to middle end of the price range (up to £4.50), Loire whites if marked as demi-sec, Johannisberg Riesling from the United States and many wines described as Rhine Riesling from the southern hemisphere. Orvieto Abboccato from Italy is another alternative. Few reds will suit unless you can reduce your sugar intake. Beaujolais or some wines from individual Crus village in the region – Fleurie or Saint-Amour are examples – may be quite pleasing, especially if served slightly chilled. Also try Gamay de Touraine, or Gamay Beaujolais from California. But don't worry if reds don't suit you; just enjoy whites.

4   Anyone who takes three sugars or sweeteners
    has a really sweet palate and is likely to
    appreciate only the sweetest whites like
    Sauternes, Coteaux du Layon or Bonnezeaux,
    or those wonderful half-bottles of Austrian
    sweet delicacies from Burgenland, late-har-
    vested or botrytised New World wines and
    similar German ones rated as Auslese, or the
    very expensive Eiswein, Beerenauslese or
    Trockenbeerenauslese. Asti Martini or Rich
    Champagne would be enjoyable sparklers.

ICE BUCKETS

You don't need a thermometer to use an ice
bucket to its best advantage. Just follow some
simple guidelines.

1   Take an empty ice bucket; a metal waste
    paper bin will do in an emergency.
2   Put the wine bottle in the bucket.
3   Fill the remaining space, right to the top, with
    plenty of ice. Most leading multiple wine
    retailers now sell it by the bag; few people
    have enough in their fridge or freezer.
4   Add cold water until it is only 5 centimetres (2
    inches) from the top of the bucket. The ice
    will freeze the water which will then cover the
    surface of the bottle evenly.

Remember that if the neck of the bottle protrudes
some of the wine will not be chilled satisfactorily.
If this happens and if the bottle is relatively
inexpensive, simply invert it several times to
redistribute the wine. If it is a fine wine either
opt to take the first glassful for yourself, leaving

the coolest wine for other drinkers, or pour a small volume into each glass and share it out. Inverting Champagne or a sparkling wine is not advised.

RAPID ICE

Rapid Ice (wine chiller) sleeves are extremely practical devices and are made for both still and sparkling wines. Simply leave the sleeve in your freezer overnight, then slide it over a bottle for five or six minutes. The contents will then be perfectly chilled.

Can You Remember?

1 What size is a Jeroboam of Champagne?

2 Which Champagne house produces a prestige label called La Grande Dame?

3 Which Sherry house was founded by Paddy Murphy?

4 What is Ottrott?

5 Give the dates of Prohibition.

6 Who is the only teetotal winemaker in the world?

7 Where was the first vineyard in the United States located?

8 Which wine won the 'Least Inspired Label' award?

9 What is the oldest wine on regular sale?

10 Who brought Barcelona to a standstill?

11 Who is the patron saint of wine producers?

12 Which vintage Madeira did Napoleon buy but never drink?

13 Who said 'Take a little wine for the sake of your digestion'?

14 Which vines are unpopular with baboons?

15 Name the most important grape in the Sherry region.

16 Who was the Champagne Führer?

17 What is a *galet*?

18 Which Shakespearean character loved to drink sack?

19 What are *zapatos*?

20 Which winery was the first in the Barossa Valley?

The answers can be found on the following pages:

1: page 84; **2**: page 108; **3**: page 18; **4**: page 5; **5**: page 78; **6**: page 35; **7**: page 39; **8**: page 71; **9**: page 47; **10**: pages 25–6; **11**: page 54; **12**: page 62; **13**: page 67; **14**: page 87; **15**: page 93; **16**: page 16; **17**: page 121; **18**: pages 131–132; **19**: page 143; **20**: page 15.